ABOUT THE A

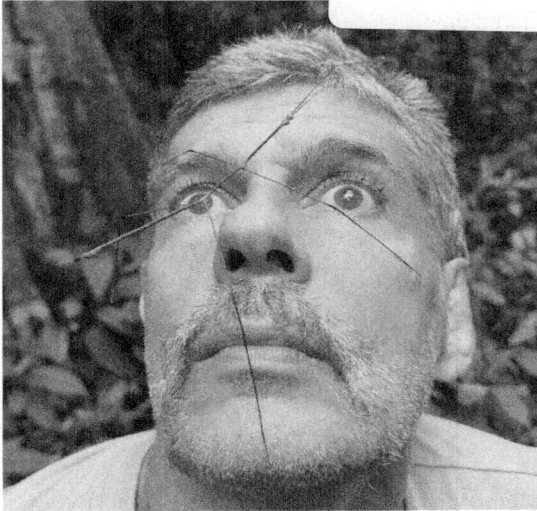

This is Wayne's first book. He was born in New Zealand in 1967. Reached his Financial Freedom at age 40 and retired at 43. Wayne left for the UK in 1990, aged 22, for a 2-year OE (overseas experience), but somehow, that 2 years has turned into 34 years with no sign of ending. Waynes had some serious career focus along the way, but he was also able to throw into that chapter of life a 2.5-year backpacking adventure. Having lived in Asia for the last 26 years (Hong Kong, Singapore, and now Thailand), Wayne feels very connected to the beautiful vibe of Asia. These days, life is a mix of outdoor nature stuff (hiking, trail running, cycling, and tennis) and a bit of nerdy spreadsheet stuff to keep the brain ticking over (cool brain versus idiot brain type stuff). When not in Thailand, he typically travels off the beaten path, having been to 100+ countries (with many more travel adventures planned). The picture is of a stick insect crawling on his face – creep crawly insects don't freak him out at all!

FINANCIAL FREEDOM

SH!T NO ONE TEACHES US

Why didn't anyone teach me this? Arrrgghhhh!!!!

This book will guide **YOU** on how to achieve **YOUR** Financial Freedom. If I had this book when I started my journey, then it would've been a lot easier.

Let's hope I can make Financial Freedom a lot easier for **YOU**.

By Wayne Sweet

Please note that I am not a financial adviser, and nothing I write in this book should be taken as financial advice. Always make sure you do your own due diligence on anything investment-related. This book and the information provided within is for entertainment purposes only.

Note that I haven't written this with AI. I just used a few internet searches where I referenced them, and there is some Leonardo AI on the cover and at the end of the book.

Please note no AI was hurt while making this book.

Table of Contents

INTRODUCTION

Financial Freedom Planning – Shit no one teaches us.

I originally wanted to call this Financial Freedom - Shit we don't learn at school. But unfortunately, the 'shit we don't learn at school' banner had already been used.

However, it's not just limited to school stuff, it's also:

Shit we don't learn at University.

Shit we don't learn from family.

Shit we don't learn from any other formal sort of education.

Keeping it relevant.

It's typically just stuff we pick up along the way, which really sucks because it's super important and relevant for everyone. It's a lot more important than learning about Pythagoras' theory on triangles, and it's a lot more relevant than learning Calculus (I haven't measured the angle of a triangle since high school maths, and I have no idea who or what Calculus got up to).

I would love to go back in time and challenge my high school economics teacher as to why this stuff was never taught (although he did teach me about Maslow's law of diminishing returns), but then I guess if he knew the stuff himself, he wouldn't have taught economics until he was in his 60s (unless he was one of the few who found a job they are really passionate about). Same challenge for my math teacher, too!

Spreading the message.

Unfortunately, Financial Freedom is stuff we should learn, but we rarely do. Why not?

Some (way too many) people never pick it up and are never exposed to it.

Some may pick up bits of it here and there and never put it to practice; it just passes them by.

Some believe that they've left it too late, so they just don't bother.

Some simply don't give a shit.

Some people just don't want to learn.

I have done a few one-on-one or small group sessions around the kitchen table (for free – never charged for it), and although we all have different ways of learning and taking stuff in, there have been a few when clearly it's just not their thing (lights are on but nobody's home syndrome).

A few months ago, I met up with a couple of 20-year-olds (friends of friends) at a cafe. They are currently in University. I asked them why they were at University/why they wanted to work, and the answer was basically "to get a job to earn money." I gave them my high-level 'elevator pitch' on my Financial Freedom thingy and encouraged them to follow up with me for a 3-hour (free) session on how to reach Financial Freedom. I still haven't heard back from them. It's odd because if someone offered me a 3-hour free session to get ahead financially, I would jump at the opportunity, especially if I am spending over 4 years at University to "get a job to earn money." Maybe I didn't present myself very well or need to work on my elevator pitch more.

Keep it simple.

There is a lot of stuff out there on growing wealth, but it's often presented as quite academic – fortunately, I am not very academic, phew! And please ignore all the 'hype' content on YouTube, etc., mainly about getting super RICH (puke spew). There is often a fast red sports car in the background and a swimming pool and some bling-bling, and I just think to myself, "Super Cringey."

I hope this book provides a more practical common sense approach to reaching your Financial Freedom – with some fun anecdotes along the way, as learning is meant to be fun. Perhaps you already know most of this stuff (it aint rocket science), and that's cool - hopefully, it provides you with a "cool, I know that shit already moment."

It will be key to understanding your own style and working out what's best for you. No real major 'must stick to the recipe.' Tweak it as best for you and also based on what circumstances may come your way later down the track.

My life in < 162 words.

Before we get started, here is my brief bio: I will provide plenty of examples of how I personally used some of the guiding principles in various chapter content, followed by a more long-winded spiel at the end. (My dad was a little bit of a show-off, so I do get a little uncomfortable at times talking too much about myself. I am mindful not to do it too much.)

<162 words:

Born in New Zealand in 1967.

Started working aged 18 in I.T.

Left for the UK at age 22 – an opportunity to earn better money and travel.

Backpacked for 2.5 years (Middle East/Africa/Asia) from about 24 to 26ish.

Back working in the UK at age 27.

Aged 30 - 42 Transferred to Hong Kong with work and then Singapore and then back to Hong Kong and then back to Singapore.

Aged 40. Financial Freedom realised. But I am still working, and it is nice to have a bit more financial breathing space. And I wasn't hating work YET! I didn't work between the ages of 39 and 41.

Aged 43. I quit work! I am retired. FINANCIAL FREEDOM WOOOHOOO!

Aged 57 (as I type this) – I'm still enjoying my Financial Freedom/Retirement. I live in Thailand.

I have been married twice (yikes) but have no kids (hmmm, does that make me an environmentalist???)

I am content!

How many years do you want to work for?

I worked for about 21 years - which I am very pleased with. Later, I will provide you with some 'career hacks' that worked really well for me. At the time, I didn't know they were going to be so beneficial, and they weren't really hacks; they were just things that played out well for me over time. And it's easier to look back at key turning events in life and think," Yep, that's exactly how I planned it," but the reality, unfortunately, is that it may not be the case. Our 'idiot brain' does like to trick us at times that we are awesomely smart – well, idiot brain, it's time you started to listen to me!!

If you are thinking, 'NO WAY am I going to work for 21 years – that's way too long - stuff that,' then I hope this book helps to provide you with some perspective on how quickly time actually moves and why appreciating that is super important for Financial Freedom planning. Yep, you can hopefully achieve your Financial Freedom quicker, BUT to do that, you need a plan, and you will need to balance risk with reward. Oh, and you need luck, but sometimes we create our own luck.

Here's some context on the challenges faced by most:

- Less than 1% retire before age 50.
- 50% retire between the ages of 61 and 65.
- 70% retire by age 66.
- 11% are still working past age 75.

Above is based on the U.S.A. I'm not sure about your home country, but these *stats probably don't vary too much on a global basis.

The following shows the average amount saved by age group in the UK (as of Jan 2024).

AGE GROUP	AVERAGE SAVINGS
18 - 24	£3,636
25 -34	£3,748
35 - 44	£5,714
45 - 54	£9,402
55 - 73	£18,245
74+	£36,940

Those sitting on the average in the 35+ age group have a very long and tough road to achieving Financial Freedom. They will likely never achieve it unless they are ready to make some very uncomfortable decisions.

*Note that 67% of all statistics are made up: hmmmm oooops, make that 72% of all statistics are made up!

How old is old?

If you are young and think I am too old to be giving relevant advice (which I would've when I was younger), please don't write me off as some old, out-of-touch dude (is 'dude' a really old term? Ooops!). 57 is still quite young – assuming I will live until 90, then I am kinda halfway between 20 and 90 years old (I assume I will die around 90'ish assuming there is no new technology that makes me a cyber-dude – oh, if that's the case I may run out of $$$$ yikes). Maybe BOTOX LIPS will be back in fashion for the 8th time by 2060??

I hope I have a somewhat young perspective on most stuff. I have travelled to over 100+ countries, and I enjoy following current social issues and future technologies and learning how they may impact the road ahead. One of my more recent trips was a solo motorbike (rental) ride from Delhi to Ladakh to Delhi – just awesome (apart from the pickup truck that wiped me out = cut my knee = scar = another tattoo of life).

Confession: I can't name a single Taylor Swift song: not sure if I win or lose points for that confession.

The best age group for this book is **everyone**. Never too early or too late to learn about Financial Freedom. Don't fall for the 'I missed the financial boat thingy," as this book will hopefully illustrate that making some uncomfortable decisions and the power of patience and compounding can really help to get things back on track. **I wish I had this book when I was a teenager!**

The book format.

The first half of the book focuses on 39 guiding principles. Most are self-explanatory, but as it is a book, I will expand on them; otherwise, I will be publishing a 15-page PowerPoint presentation instead (and Amazon doesn't publish them). Some are brief, and some are a bit more detailed with personal examples. As they are guidelines, use them to suit your personal style.

The mechanics of the plan (I am a bit of a spreadsheet nerd) are important, but I think the guidelines are needed to provide the correct context before tackling the expense tracker and the Financial Freedom roadmap.

What to invest in follows next, as the 39 guidelines and nerdy spreadsheets are key for setting the scene for what, when, and how to invest. These are my personal takes based on my own experience - I reference doing your own 'due diligence' a lot in this book as that's a key requirement to all investing.

The last section of the book is more about navigating one's career and a lot of my own personal experience. It's important because the better the career, the better the opportunity to save more money and then the quicker you can get your money working for **YOU**!

There are also a couple of examples of the 'opportunity cost of bad habits,' for example, cigarettes – it's a bit mind-blowing.

Then, I finish off with some other random topics that I think are very relevant to Financial Freedom and life in general. The approach to achieving Financial Freedom is pretty much the same for Wellness, Fitness and Adventure goals, etc.

I hope my writing style (and humour are OK). I don't try to be funny – it just kinda comes naturally. And if you don't find me funny, that's OK – (maybe I am just weird) – as there's lots of very serious, relevant content to help get you where you want to be.

Note: As a Kiwi, many global swear words aren't considered swear words, so when I use words like 'shit' and 'piss' please don't be offended – I just don't consider them as swear words – I consider them as beautiful words of expression (note, if you are a YouTuber in front of the fast red sports car going bling-bling - when I call you 'Super Cringey' there are actually other words I am internally swearing at you).

Remember, I am not a financial adviser, and nothing I write in this book should be taken as financial advice. Always make sure you do your own due diligence on anything investment-related. This book and the information provided within is for entertainment purposes only. (OK, that's got me off the hook – phew!!).

Righto, let's get on with it.

39 GUIDING PRINCIPLES – IN NO PARTICULAR ORDER.

(Why 39 principles = because not everything in life has to be rounded up).

Apply what works for you. Make sure you maintain **balance** to maintain progress and enjoyment.

Maslow's law of diminishing returns = (my simple definition) the more you have something, the less of a buzz you get from it, simple example: Super-hot day, and you have just finished a run, you knock back a really cold Coca-Cola. That Coca-Cola was so awesome – you really needed that. You knock back a second Coca-Cola – that was really good but not as good as the first one. But then you knock back a third Coca-Cola – well, that was the plan, but halfway through, it just didn't give you any kick, so you just drink it nice and slow, and you don't bother getting a fourth one. You can apply this to a lot of things in life!

1. Don't use the word RICH. It means nothing.

I hate the word RICH (spew puke yuck) when it comes to Financial Freedom. It's a stupid word with almost zero relevance. We stereotype it with bling bling and big houses and fast red sports cars (Super Cringey) and lots of fancy pantsy stuff and success. It isn't something that can be defined - as being rich in one country may not equal being rich in another country, and being rich doesn't mean you are a nice person. Rich, to me, equals a superficial, non-relevant status symbol. In my 100+ countries of travel, I have met many awesome, amazing people and many of them are not doing very well financially. I have also met many awesome, amazing people who seem to be doing very well financially. And unfortunately, I have met quite a few 'perceived RICH' typically self-entitled arses.

I have never focused on being rich. Am I rich today? I don't give the label any thought at a personal level because I simply couldn't give a shit. I never give much thought to others I know (old school friends/ex-colleagues, etc.) on whether they are RICHER than me or not. It's irrelevant cause I know people with a lot more money than me, and I think I am a lot more content. I also know people with a lot less money than me, and they seem very content – so it's a measure that is pretty much meaningless but is marketed as something to be chased. It's a little like measuring SUCCESS as well. How can you tell if someone is more successful than someone else? It all comes down to individual perspective, and only the individual has insight into their own measure of success. Personally, I think I have done OK for myself, but then some strangers I have met along the way have quickly pointed out how empty I must feel (and I have even been called a very bad man) because I don't have children. And yet, on the flip side, not having children is a **non-**achievement I am personally very pleased with. There really is no right or wrong – only lots of complicated, different personal perspectives. (OK, there are probably some extreme outliers on success versus non-success, and that mainly covers criminals. But then maybe the kid caught up in gangs from a young age and spends 10 years in prison – gets released from prison and becomes a positive community mentor to young kids to stay out of gangs - I would likely focus on his success to learn and grow.)

It's a little like being famous, too. I haven't really ever met anyone famous, and I don't care to. I honestly can't think of anyone famous who I could meet, and I would be in awe of. I have given this a lot of thought, and I am fairly positive I would simply greet them the same way as any other stranger and have a normal, down-to-earth, equal-footing chat with them. If they tried to project their 'Oh, but I am famous, so you should respect me," I think I would just call them an arse and walk off.

This is also a little bit like "I should respect my elders." Yep, I do respect my elders, but no more than I respect my youngers – I respect everyone equally until they give me a reason not to respect them.

The point of this with rich people and successful people is I don't see the need to carry potential insecurities by comparing myself to any other people. This is important as it means you can focus on achieving Financial Freedom based on your terms without all the silly noise projected by Rich this and Rich that. More on this a little later.

OK, hopefully (maybe needs a word search later), the word RICH (spew puke yuck) will not appear in this book again. Please delete it from your Financial Freedom vocabulary.

What does all this have to do with Financial Freedom? Let's cover this in the next guiding principle.

2. Financial Freedom means different things to different people - what does it mean for you?

Financial Freedom can be considered as (thanks Google) *finding yourself in a financial position where you don't need to work unless you want to.*

You are in control of your finances and your life choices.

How do you define Financial Freedom? For you, it might mean that you don't have to go to work anymore, or you can take a lower-paying or non-paying job to do something you love. It might mean knowing that you always have a roof over your head.

For some, it means that you own your house and your cars outright. You don't have debt. That might be what you need. Others might say they need to know that they have a certain amount of income coming in and are not reliant on others so that they can travel the world without worrying about paying bills.

Still others might want to fund charities, do volunteer work, or give money to help others. There are no wrong answers, but we do need a destination. Think about what it means to you to be financially free. Once you know what it means to you, it's time to calculate how to accomplish it.

Financial Freedom does not equal RXXX (Yep, I just made it a swear word!!). What it means for you personally actually needs quite a bit of internal thinking, and the cool thing about it is that it never needs an exact answer. And it's something that will most likely continue to evolve. How would I have answered what Financial Freedom means to me at different ages? Maybe as follows:

Aged 5: To be able to eat as much ice cream as I want at any time for the rest of my life. What's Financial Freedom????

Aged 15: Still eating ice cream but flying around in my own private jet buying ice cream all over the world. Retired at 30.

Aged 25: Not really a private jet type guy anymore, so a big house, swimming pool, fast red sports car (Super Cringey), and some ice cream now and then. I need enough money and enough breathing space for my expected lifestyle to retire at 40.

Aged 35: Medium-sized house – no bad debt and enough passive income to eat out a lot (with ice cream for dessert) and travel comfortably. Enough money with enough breathing space for my expected lifestyle to retire at 45.

Aged 45: Apartment living (no lawns to mow/no pets to feed), debt free, generating semi-steady income to support a humbler lifestyle in a warm, safe, friendly environment, and being very content until the age of 80. Still eating some ice cream. Enough money with enough breathing space for my expected lifestyle to remain retired and never have to work again (unless by choice).

Aged 55: Apartment living, debt-free, generating a steady income to support a humbler lifestyle in a warm, safe, friendly environment that will see me living very contently and healthy to the age of 90. Still eating some ice cream. Retired and never have to work again (unless by choice).

Aged 65: Not sure yet, but it will be pretty close to the following: "Apartment living, debt free, generating a steady income to support a humbler lifestyle in a warm, safe, friendly environment that will see me living very contently and healthy to the age of 90+." Retired and never have to work again (unless by choice). Still eating ice cream!

And so, for me personally, my outlook on what would make me content (I will explain happy vs. content next) changed as I had more life experience and recognised what things positively push my buttons the most.

For example, while living in Hong Kong (early 30s), I was still playing rugby and enjoyed going out with the lads, getting a bit drunk and partying... but I was getting slowly bored of that and needed a change. To take peer pressure off me for not partying with the lads, I signed up to do the Macau marathon. The lads didn't hassle me whenever I said I wasn't going out that night as I had training early in the morning! It turned out I really enjoyed getting up on a Saturday and Sunday (no hangover) and joining my new running mates. Training was sometimes a 3-hour run over the hills on Saturday morning starting at 0600 and then a game of rugby at 1430pm. My marathon goal was under 4 hours, and I finished the marathon in 3 hours 36 minutes, which I was stoked with, and that became a slow ending to me going out drinking. The years that followed saw me do more and more events (triathlons/adventure races, etc.) and drink less and less. I stopped drinking any alcohol about 8 years ago - it is just not my thing anymore. I don't miss it; I don't feel like I gave anything up, and I don't see myself ever drinking again. I would never have guessed that path back when I was in my early 20s. By not drinking - does it make me boring?? I don't know, and I don't really care, but it saves me a lot of money!!

A similar experience with expensive restaurants – these days they just aren't my thing. My favourite meal experience is the local Saturday market, sitting on the ground, sharing parts of my meal with 2 friendly stray dogs. It's good to be humble!

Staying in a 5-star hotel does nothing for me – I am happy enough in a clean, quiet 1 or 2-star hotel. When I travel on an adventure, I sometimes stay in hostel dorms. When I first experienced 5-star hotels with work, I used to think they were cool - but the more I spent in them, the less they gave me any buzz (Maslow's law) - so it was good I got them out of my system. Or maybe I have tricked myself into believing that they don't add any happy value to me because I now had to pay for them myself (big respect to my idiot brain).

In essence, the magic target for Financial Freedom changed as I got older, and my lifestyle wants (versus needs) changed. The main thing is really knowing about the person you are and what your spending patterns are likely to be.

It's essentially working out:

How many years have I got left? I assume I will live to 90. If I live longer, then that's OK- so long as I manage medical expenses and can afford a rest home. Maybe there will be some really cool robot technologies to help me out. But my plan does not assume my money runs to ZERO the day I die (although that would be cool).

If I live to 90, then how much money do I require per year to provide the lifestyle I need/want? I need to factor in inflation and have enough buffer in case something unexpected hits me (e.g., a metaphorical bus = medical bills), or I live a lot longer, e.g., until 100. But I also get to add to this the passive income I generate (and grow) while not working (e.g., rent/stock dividends).

We will expand on this later, but the key takeaway from this is to spend time assessing what sort of things in life really make you content and ensure you position yourself with the Financial Freedom to live it.

Since I retired, my net $$$ equity gain has easily surpassed inflation, so I feel comfortable and have enough breathing space to meet my plans.

How much $$$ is needed for Financial Freedom? Check out the Financial Freedom road map at the end of the guideline section.

3. Happiness versus Contentment.

I will make this quick as this is a financial-focused book, but I probably changed my outlook about 20 years ago and focused as much on being Content as I did on seeking Happiness. Happiness kinda reflects peaks and troughs. It's very hard to maintain the peaks, and they can set unrealistic continual goal chasing. So, I settled on Contentment. It is really cool as it reflects more of a straight line with smaller deltas between the peaks and troughs, and it's a very satisfying feeling.

I still have many awesome experiences and not too many super shit experiences – I don't really feel like I am chasing anything super super big. I am CONTENT!

And don't fall into the trap of measuring happiness by what those around you (may) have. They appear to have more so by default human nature assumes they are happier. Thats not a good metric to use!

An interesting example: Nowadays, we have so much cool technology that those in the 1970s would have been envious of us. Are we happier today with all our awesome technology than those from the 1970s, who had a phone stuck to the wall inside the house? Who knows? How to compare?

Maybe check out Steve Cutts's "Happiness" video on YouTube: it's a bit exaggerated but has a very powerful message on chasing "Happiness."

4. Create a personal Financial Freedom plan and maintain it FOREVER!

Did you know that 75% of those who write and track their goals achieve their goals? I am not sure how accurate that statistic is given that 61% of all statistics are made up – but without a doubt, writing down your goals is a much surer way to ensure you achieve them. If written down, you have a reference point and a measurement. If not written down, then goals kind of float around in the air, and before you know it, time has passed, and those goals have been missed. This is true for all goals and not just financial goals. I first created my personal Financial Freedom plan in 1996 (age 29) – I know this date because my spreadsheet has a sheet page for every year since 1996. When I look back at the sheets from 1996 to 2024, the sheet layout has changed quite a bit since when I first started. However, the basis has always been the same.

Essentially, what is tracked:

- What is my net worth (equity) on January 1st of the new year?
- What is my forecasted savings for the calendar year (net income from salary and other investments)?
- What is my targeted net worth (equity) for December 31st?
- When will I die?
- When can I retire?

I update my spreadsheet monthly (sometimes quarterly if not much has changed in my portfolio or if I am travelling). It only took me about 2 hours to set up my initial spreadsheet back in 1996.

It takes me about 2 hours maximum to roll over the sheet from the old year to the new year.

It takes me about 1-hour maximum each month to update my spreadsheet.

For roughly 14 hours spread over a year, I keep my Financial Freedom plan updated. This keeps me focused and on track and significantly increases my % of hitting my goals. 14 hours/year = not a lot of time spent for a very large return. 14 hours = maybe the time taken to binge-watch a Netflix season?

OR

8 hours per day x 5 days per week x 46 weeks worked per year = 1840 hours working for money per year. Why not allocate 14 additional hours (0.007%) to how you can make your money work better for you?

My financial goals may vary through the years/decades, but that's to be expected.

But my financial goals are never too far from my thought process.

Oddly enough, sometimes I look back at my different yearly sheets, which also help to tell a historic storyboard. For example, when did I buy and sell a certain property, and did I make money from it? What happened to me during a certain "financial crisis," and, more importantly, how well have my finances grown since I stopped working?

Sometimes, I have friends who are having some challenges making certain decisions (life or work-related), or maybe they are super stressed. Essentially, the fuzzy fuzzy brain is sneaky. I find this is typically something a pen and paper or a few cells in a spreadsheet can fix. I get them to write down their options and look at the pros and cons, and it's interesting to see how much calmer they are after this.

I also put down non-financial goals at the beginning of each year. More on this later.

5. Make decisions based on numbers – NOT EMOTION.

I strongly support learning to use Excel or Google Sheets. Super helpful for creating/managing your personal financial plan and super helpful as you can run all sorts of various "what if" scenarios or 'stretch test" some scenarios. However, what I have found the most useful element of being confident in spreadsheets (I am an Excel guy) is that I have learned to think like a spreadsheet. What does that mean? Am I an AI robot? Not Yet!

Whenever I meet someone and they start to tell me about a financial opportunity, I ask questions designed to complete the blank Excel spreadsheet that's in my head. Basically, what data points do I need to collect to create a quick spreadsheet to see if this opportunity is worth further investigation or not? When I get back to my laptop within 5 minutes, I can crunch the numbers into a spreadsheet and determine if it is worth pursuing or not. If yes, then what's the next level of information I need to gather – basically peeling back the onion?

So long as I approach this and my own financial planning using numbers/spreadsheets, then it really helps me assess new opportunities and my current roadmap based on financial supporting data and not on emotion. Some emotions are important when evaluating financials, but they should never lead – they should always follow.

Property is a good example. I created a very simple spreadsheet for New Zealand-based properties to determine the ideal buy price to match the ideal rent ratio (positive cash flow needed). I needed to take into consideration the following:

- Buy price.
- Renovation costs.
- Legal costs.

- Property tax (sales and income and capital gains).
- Deposit amount.
- Loan amount.
- Interest rate repayments.
- Council rates.
- Insurance costs.
- Miscellaneous maintenance costs.
- Expected rent.
- Agent fees.
- % breathing space to protect me in case interest rates go up, rents go down, etc.

When I went to look at a potential property to purchase (to rent out), I weeded out the ones that wouldn't meet my ROI (Return on Investment) criteria and focused on the ones that would. Property = investment first!

My current apartment is my home, and it needed renovating, but I made sure (even though it's my home) that my renovation costs would not exceed the value added to the potential future market price. No point decorating walls in a commissioned Mona Lisa mural that might cost $1000s when the new potential owner might hate Mona Lisa and would see no value in the renovation and would paint it back to white. I will share some nice, simple tips on adding to a property value later.

In more recent years, I have helped a few friends by putting together a financial business plan for some new business they are thinking of setting up. It's quite interesting because I don't even have any knowledge of the business (e.g., a veterinarian hospital), but Excel and I seem to find a way to relatively easily put together a detailed financial plan to help ensure that the right decisions are made (based on numbers and not on emotion).

Important Note: you **don't** have to be an advanced spreadsheet – basic is good enough!

Important Note: Numbers in a spreadsheet help to manage 'idiot brain' into being 'practical common-sense brain." That's a much better approach to making financial decisions.

Side Note: COMMON SENSE is a good life skill to acquire.

Google says that common sense isn't something you are born with, but rather something you learn through life experiences and observations.

If you feel you may lack a bit of common sense at times, then my common sense says you should make an effort to learn a bit more common sense (but I am not sure exactly how that is done).

6. Professional Financial Advisers ALWAYS(?) have a product to sell.

OK, statistically, it may not be ALWAYS, but it certainly will be almost always, so make sure when you meet with them that you have got your Bullshit detection radar on. Over the years, I have talked to a few, and it's quite interesting to get a gauge on what's out there as potential investment opportunities. However, just remember that financial advisers have a portfolio of products that they need to sell, and they typically cannot sell everything. On a few occasions, the financial adviser led the conversation by assessing my amount to invest, my risk profile, etc., and then it came across as a little cliched: "Have I got just the right product for you?" That's not to say that it is the wrong product – but that's not to say that it is the right product, either.

Financial advisers also add a management fee as well. It can easily vary from 0.75 to 1.8% management fee per annum, which you pay even if your investment goes negative. As you will see in 'compounding returns' a little later, these fees can add up over time. A common product sold by financial advisers is mutual funds or a portfolio of stocks. There are very few statistics to support that actively managed mutual funds 'beat the market,' yet they have the management fees on top. Various searches on the internet indicate that fewer than 15% of professional finance advisers beat the market long term – that's a pretty poor win rate to be adding a fee to.

"Beat the market" in this book will simply refer to performing better than the S&P 500 (this being the top 500 companies on the U.S. stock exchange). You can buy an S&P 500 ETF yourself directly with no financial adviser with an annual expense ratio (same as a management fee) of 0.03%. More on stocks/ ETFs and markets and portfolios later in this book. Paying 0.03% versus 1% is a huge difference over time.

Sometimes, financial advisers may be good as a way to get started or evaluate your own investment style. I am not poo-pooing them outright. Simply do your due diligence and have your bullshit radar on and remember this:

NO ONE CARES MORE ABOUT YOUR MONEY THAN YOU DO! Please remember this – it is important when coming to money management opportunities.

Please, please, please don't forget that NO ONE CARES MORE ABOUT YOUR MONEY THAN YOU DO!

HOT OF THE PRESS: SEPT 2024. Maybe not that hot by the time you read this, but a friend of mine coincidentally mentioned to me that he was getting some feedback sessions from a financial adviser he had engaged with directly. He didn't know I was into Financial Freedom-type stuff, so I asked him if he would be OK sharing with me what they came back with – he didn't have to share his personal $ information. My friend is 60 and looking to retire soon.

The advisers came back with a portfolio of 12 different asset types (mutual funds, ETFs, and some bonds). It was a lengthy report, but nowhere could I see the exact items (fund or ETF code) in the portfolio (I couldn't do a deeper analysis) or, the expected growth or the expected passive income (dividends/bond coupons), or the fees of each of the 12 items. **BUT** what I could see was the financial adviser's 1.78% annual management fee. **OUCH!** (which is on top of the management fees in each of the 12 portfolio items).

We created a very simple spreadsheet, and it was sent back to the adviser last Monday to list each of the 12 items, showing us the detailed information above. This Monday (today), we got the spreadsheet back, and it's only about half completed. They still haven't answered the question on projected growth and projected income. My friend will not be using these 'professionals.'

Instead, we came up with a DIY build and manage-it-yourself solution (5 ETFs) that is balanced and diversified and with better expected growth and income (and reduced risk) with an overall management fee of < 0.15% (not my fee – I am free – this is the fee in the ETFs). My friend just needs to be prepared to spend the time and gain the confidence that he can manage this himself – which he is! The opportunity cost for him is very big because, as you will learn in compounding interest, the 1.78% is potentially a very large amount of money over time.

Oh, out of the 12 items in the portfolio, one item was a **hedged** mutual fund, and one item was a **non-hedged** mutual fund. Pretty complicated stuff, huh? Maybe the advisers thought, "Hey, let's throw in some of this hedged stuff because it's quite complicated, and the more complicated it sounds then, the cleverer we look, and so it's a no-brainer to have us build your wealth." My personal take is the more complicated you make something when your focus should be to make it simple presents you as a very dumb (or dishonest) person.

Confession: I will hopefully sell lots of copies of this book, and hopefully, it will make me some money. This would be the first time I would have made any money from providing my insights on Financial Freedom. My kitchen table sessions have always been free, and I have always said, "I may be the only financial dude (which I am not!) who doesn't have anything to sell! By getting this book published, am I a person of zero principles or just a capitalist pig? Oink Oink!

7. Get RXXX quick =s SCAM!

Thanks to social media everywhere, we now get hit with catchphrases such as….

"How I made my first million in 2 years."

"Make big money every day."

"Getting RXXX the lazy way"

"Making money while sleeping"

"I started with nothing – now I have it all."

"I retired at 25 – you can do the same."

"This stock is going to the moon."

"Forex the easiest way to become RXXX

"I have a red fast sports car, and I am not 'Super Cringey" (OK, I made that one up!)

And on and on and on...

If you choose to watch this stuff (there are some things to be learned from some of them), make sure you have got your BULLSHIT radar on and always do your own due diligence.

The key to approaching the 'get RXXX quick blah blah blah" is to recognise that, ideally, it should play no part in your roadmap to Financial Freedom. These things are punts and should be treated as such. ALWAYS DO YOUR OWN DUE DILIGENCE.

Confession: I have played around in the past, trading FOREX, penny stocks, and even crypto trading. I have never been drawn in by the hype but always by the interest in seeing how the mechanics of this stuff works. I have only ever invested < 0.01% of my total portfolio with the expectation that this is a long shot to win. As suspected, the "magic formula" doesn't work (or is not sustainable), but the author of the "magic formula" makes money from training courses/YouTube/Patreon, etc. Generally, they need to create the NOISE to get subscribers. I am not calling them all scammers (although many are). Many appeared just after COVID-19, and after about 6 months, most of them had disappeared. Hmmmm, they either made it super RXXX and didn't need the distraction of YouTube (NOT!) OR, most likely, they couldn't sustain the NOISE and the "magic formula" shit itself – wow, what a surprise! I think the latter to be true.

8. It's not a sprint – it's a marathon!

At pretty much any age, you can get out of bed (ignoring the hangover) with no training and no real plan - find a bit of road or track and sprint 100 to 200 metres. Your time to complete it may be good (or not), but you will, in high probability, have completed it (and hopefully didn't fall over and injure yourself).

At pretty much any age, you can **NOT** get out of bed with no training and no real plan - find a bit of road or track and run a marathon (42.195 km). You will not be able to complete the distance. If you try this without a plan, you will almost certainly fail. You will certainly need to walk some of it. You will almost certainly injure yourself. (OK, there may be a few statistical outliers who could achieve this, but they are rare).

To reach Financial Freedom on your terms, you need to have a plan. The quicker you try to achieve this, the more risk you may be adding. Adding risk is fine so long as you account for it in your plan.

9. Time goes quicker than you may realise. Patience is key.

When I was about 15, I wanted to retire at 30. When I got to 30, I realised at the age of 15 I had pretty much no concept of time.

When I was 17, my mother died. She was 53. When I was 17, I thought that was a little young; however, I also thought 53 was quite old. As I was reaching 50, I realised, WOW, 53 is so young. I was so wrong. Mum died young.

When I bought my first rental property at about 31, there was a 20-year mortgage. That meant potentially that the mortgage wouldn't be paid off until about 51 years old. Wow, that seemed so far away. Turned out it wasn't!

When I was 40, I could've retired and was ready to retire, but I figured I would work 2 more years to create some breathing space. That 2 years went super quick.

During Covid, I felt the 2 years were the quickest ever. They weren't. 2 years = 2 years. I read recently that time seems to go quicker if you actually do nothing/achieve nothing/have no major highlights to look back on.

These days, I feel as if time is going quicker than ever before. Is it because I am older (or not doing much)?

I am now 57, and I think maybe I will live to be 90. I have a whopping 34 years left. 34 years ago, I was 22. When I think of being 22, I think that was quite some time ago, but I also think, hmmm, actually, it wasn't that long ago. When I think around about 90, I will be dead – sometimes I think that's going to take forever, and other times I think, hmmm, that's going to come around quickly.

Basically, we struggle to have a real concept of how quickly time passes. My advice is not to get too hung up on the "but that's going to take forever" mindset because, fortunately (or unfortunately), it won't. Build things into your roadmap, plan accordingly, and be patient. Don't force stuff that doesn't need to be forced (without doing a little risk-reward assessment).

The reality is that time is still going at the same speed as time has always done.

OK, enough about time, as it's now time for the next one!

10. GREED is a killer.

"I want it all, and I want it now" - Freddy Mercury and Queen!

The quicker we want IT, the more risk we must take to achieve IT. (whatever IT is?) I have no problem with that approach so long as it's executed as part of a plan with realistic expectations and balanced risk assessment, and if it doesn't work out, then learn from it and take accountability for it. Chasing things based on greed will almost inevitably result in shortcuts being taken. When shortcuts back-fire then they become longcuts – you need more time to get back to your pre-Greed starting point. Chasing Financial Freedom based on GREED isn't a good formula.

During COVID, I bought some speculator stocks. Some of them went up really high (100%+ gain) really fast, but I didn't sell them because I thought they would go up and up and up. Well they didn't! They went down and down and down faster than they went up and instead of being up 100+% I ended up being down 50%+ from my initial investment. There were no fundamentals to support this price rise – only noise and hype and noise and hype. Some stocks have recovered and I have sold them at break even. Some are yet to recover and I am waiting to sell them once they get back to break even.

BUT

My greed was measured. I only speculated with a very small % of my portfolio. I took a measured risk – it didn't work out – no big deal as the other 99% of my portfolio was never exposed to the GREED.

11. Kiss your EGO goodbye!

This ties in directly with RXXX and Greed and the 'Game of Life.'

The bigger your ego the more money you will 'waste' keeping it inflated.

If you have a bit of an ego, when you build your Financial Freedom plan, make sure you add in some extra years to achieve it. Why? Because egos can be very expensive.

'Bling bling look at me, aren't I cool, with my designer clothes/pricey watches/expensive shoes/new car? = NO NOT REALLY!

Remember, the person who cares most about what you look like in the mirror is you! The many minor details that you look at just aren't noticeable to others.

When I was a teenager, I was probably a bit of a show-off on some things (remember, my dad was a little bit of a show-off, so I guess that's where I learnt it from). But fortunately, I used to observe my dad and his ways (he loved to talk about all the awesome stuff he was doing - which wasn't that awesome – only awesome to him), and at some point, I realised being a show-off to inflate my own ego simply made me present myself as a bit of a dick.

I do recognise there are some cultural differences here between certain parts of the world, and it is something I have noticed, having grown up in New Zealand and lived in Asia (Hong Kong, Singapore, Thailand, for the past 23 years). The following are just my general experiences, and that doesn't mean they reflect on everyone:

In New Zealand and Australia, we have what's called the "tall poppy syndrome," which basically means if someone starts to be successful, they are often cut down a few pegs – i.e. discouraged from succeeding by those around them. The advantage of this

31

approach is that it can help to keep the EGO in check. The disadvantage of this approach is it can smother success. The way around this is pretty simple – chase your goals/be successful and do it in a humble manner.

What I like about New Zealand and Australia is that you often don't know who has the money, and therefore, people are mostly treated on a level playing field. Walk into the local corner store "dairy" in a scruffy t-shirt, rugby shorts and bare feet, and you will likely get the same level of customer service welcome as someone arriving with a suit and tie and nice shoes on. That's pretty cool.

In Singapore quite a few years back, a local Singaporean friend of a friend told me that maybe she wasn't going to send her son to Australia for University because they did not seem very welcoming and friendly. I highlighted to her in a polite manner that in the past 30 minutes that we had been talking, she had let me know which street she had her house (not an apartment) on, what car she drove, what her favourite watch was, etc.; she was dropping her wealth indicators into the conversation to try and impress me and support her Ego. In some Asian cultures, what she had done would have earned her quiet, unassuming respect. I highlighted to her that in Australia, it would not - it would label her typically as quite showy, ego-centric and, therefore, a little boring. I indicated that this may be why she is not widely received in Australia in a welcoming, friendly manner.

Just to summarise this point = Kiss Your Ego Goodbye!

12. Consumerism: Needs vs Wants – It's all just STUFF!

This ties in nicely with Kiss Your Ego Goodbye!

We are constantly bombarded with buy this and buy this and buy this and buy this and buy this – more than ever before, thanks to social media being everywhere. I call it the BRAND TRAP!

When we are teenagers, I guess the Brand Trap focuses mainly on clothes and devices. We get a bit older than it starts to focus on cars and classy restaurants/wines/hotels, and if we don't keep it in check, it extends to expensive holidays and really expensive homes, and without stopping to think about it, you have wasted a shit load of money on STUFF. Yep, 90% of it is just STUFF and too much STUFF. Everything we buy has an opportunity cost, and I will provide a few cool examples later on cigarettes, the coffee fix, cars, etc.).

If you want to achieve Financial Freedom earlier, then start challenging your idiot brain to see if you really (really?) need to buy this particular thing or not!

And make sure you understand the opportunity cost of your consumer behaviour. Does it give you a long-term sense of satisfaction or just a 'quick fix' sense of that's a cool buzz, but I want more and more and more? (Remember what Maslow had to say about this). Find your balance!!

Fortunately, I have never fallen into the BRAND TRAP. When work provided my phone, it was an Apple. When my phone packed in after work, I bought a Huawei, and now I have a RealMe. Awesome camera and specification. It's just a lot cheaper. How much of the latest technology do I really need? How much am I willing to pay for that extra 0.25 GB of storage or that extra 10 minutes of charging time? I would hate to be defined by people I know (or don't know) by what phone brand I use. I do a lot of running (road and trail), so maybe I will go through 4 pairs of running shoes per year. I buy Decathlon shoes because they are just as good and a lot cheaper than, say, Nike. I dress cleanly, but I couldn't tell you what brand my clothes are (probably fake knockoffs). I am proud to say I have never owned an expensive designer handbag. If you are going to judge me by what brand I wear, then we probably aren't going to have a great deal in common. I have sometimes wondered if I was female, if I would wear make-up, or how much I would spend on it. As I got older, I seemed to become more and more of a minimalist, which I quite like. Too much STUFF is a waste of money, a distraction in life and a bit of a bore after a while. **Stuff is just stuff!**

Confession: I have fallen into 'buy cheap buy twice' a few times – mainly thanks to buying stuff online. I do love a bargain!

13. Smart versus Patience versus Luck.

So, if Greed, Ego and Consumerism don't necessarily help achieve early Financial Freedom, then what is a good recipe? Basically, it comes down to having a SMART plan with a PATIENT approach and getting some LUCK along the way.

"The harder I work, the luckier I get" - Mark Twain. (Yep, I have heard of him).

"The smarter I work, the luckier I get," said Wayne Sweet (Yep, I have heard of him).

When I started work, I worked hard as I didn't have the experience/knowledge at 18. Then, somewhere along the line, I could add smart to the equation. I continued to work hard and work smart combined, and that helped me a lot.

This ties in with being optimistic – but if you are too optimistic, then you will likely get caught up in the 'my shit doesn't stink' trap, so try to ensure your optimism remains checked and balanced.

Interestingly, in high-performance events/races or big gambling wins, it is very common for the winner to reference, "My training really paid off – it really made a difference."

For the person who didn't win, it is very common for them to reference, "damn, I was so close that was just bad luck. "

This is essentially our ego avoiding reality and the idiot brain doing its thing again.

Don't forget that the quicker you try to attain your Financial Freedom, the more risk you must take.

14. Higher risk profile when younger – lower risk profile when older.

As a general rule, this makes good sense.

If you stuff up a very risky investment when you are 25 years old, and you have lost your life savings, well, that is bad, but you have got many years to recover. You are young and many years ahead of you, and hopefully, this stuff up will become something you learn a lot from.

If you stuff up a very risky investment when you are 75 years old, and you have lost your life savings, well, you haven't got many years to recover. You are relatively old and not many years ahead of you. This is something you really don't want to learn from at 75.

Depending on the magnitude of the stuff up, you can typically recover over a 5-year period (if you are young). If you are old, well, you aren't likely to recover your life savings by the age of 80 unless you attempt something even more high risk than before.

When you work through your plan for Financial Freedom, check out the 'power of 5 years' on your roadmap. We will cover compounding returns later, but it is essentially having an investment and the passive income made from that investment (e.g. rents/stock dividends) is reinvested again to keep generating more income.

Once you start your career and if you can save a little more each year (assuming your salary increases but your expenses don't increase by the same amount and there is no stupid inflation), and you can invest smartly, then you can potentially target to double your net savings (equity) every 5 to 7 years.

5 years is important because it can help you fix a stuff up, or it can help you double your net savings.

Assuming you start at 20 and live until 90, then that's 14 cycles (14 x 5 years = 70 years).

Assuming you stuff everything up at 75 and live until 90, then that's only 3 cycles (3 x 5 years = 15 years). There's not much time to un-stuff the stuff up.

Consider the following:

Age	Action	Action	Action
20	work	save	invest
25	work	save	invest
30	work	save	invest
35	work	save	invest
40	work	save	invest
45	work	save	invest
50	work	save	invest
55	work	save	invest
60	retired	save	invest
65	retired	save	invest
70	retired	save	invest
75	retired	save	invest
80	retired	save	invest
85	retired	save	invest
90	retired	save	invest

The better age to stuff up is 20. You still have many 5 year cycles left

The worst age to stuff up is 55+ because you haven't got many 5 year cycles left.

The best time to stuff up is **NEVER!**

A common theme when investing in the stock market is that younger investors tend to have a portfolio of some quite higher-risk growth stocks - i.e. looking for the next Tesla, Microsoft, or Apple. As we age, we will likely rebalance that portfolio to less risky stocks that focus on paying dividends (typically quarterly income from stocks such as Coca-Cola). I personally think having that balanced portfolio at a young age is just as magic. I personally hold a mix of growth and dividend stocks/ETFs with some % (typically less than 3%) as slightly higher-risk speculator stocks. More on this later.

15. Understand Return on Investment (ROI).

ROI is simply the return that can be made on one's investment. e.g.

I invest $10k into a fixed deposit in the bank, and I get 3% interest per annum, then I get $300 as a return on my investment, so that's an ROI of 3%. But it's possible that some tax has to be paid on that interest (typically 10%), so it's actually as follows:

Investment	$10,000		
Interest	$300	3.0%	Gross return
Tax	$30	10.0%	Tax on interest
ROI	$270	2.7%	Net Return

Is 2.7% a good ROI? That really depends on how it fits into your overall plan. During the Covid pandemic, bank interest rates were pretty much at 0.5%, and in August 2023, bank interest rates in many countries were up at 5%.

Buying a rental property typically has two income streams. 1 = Rent and 2 = Capital gains as the property increases in value.

Can you buy a house, rent it out, pay interest on your mortgage, and get positive cash flow?

Will the property increase in value over the next 5 to 10 to 15 to 20+ years?

Will the positive cash flow from rent and the capital gain (over time) be greater than current bank interest rates today for the next 5 to 10 to 15 to 20+ years?

Can you manage the debt (mortgage interest repayments, as these also vary pretty much in line with bank interest rates)?

Or are you better putting your money into the stock market? And if so, which stock market and which stocks/ETFs?

Or sticking your cash under your mattress = is unlikely, as inflation is almost guaranteed!!

Before making this investment decision, you need to spend time looking at the ROI of this investment, how long your investment horizon is, and how much cash might be needed just in case this investment goes south on you.

I will cover this in more detail later, but it's important to get used to thinking of investment opportunities in terms of ROI. As mentioned before, "thinking like a spreadsheet is a cool way to think."

16. Understand the power of compounding returns.

"Compounding returns. I love it! I want to marry it "- Wayne Sweet

Some other quotes from famous people on compounding returns:

"Compound interest is the eighth wonder of the world. He who understands it earns it… he who doesn't … pays it" – Albert Einstein (Yep, heard of him).

"The Compound Effect is the principle of reaping huge rewards from a series of small, smart choices" — Darren Hardy (never heard of him).

"There will be good years, and there will be bad years, but the compounding will continue on unabated." — Pietros Maneos (never heard of him).

"Time is your friend; impulse is your enemy. Take advantage of compound interest and don't be captivated by the siren song of the market." — Warren Buffett (Yep, heard of him).

"If you understand compound interest, you basically understand the universe." — Robert Breault (never heard of him).

"Understanding both the power of compound interest and the difficulty of getting it is the heart and soul of understanding a lot of things." — Charlie Munger (Yep, heard of him).

"Time is your friend; impulse is your enemy." — John C. Bogle (Yep, heard of him).

"Enjoy the magic of compounding returns. Even modest investments made in one's early 20s are likely to grow to staggering amounts over the course of an investment lifetime." John C. Bogle (same dude as above).

"Compound interest on the debt was the banker's greatest invention, to capture, and enslave, a productive society." — Albert Einstein (Yep, him again).

OK, enough of all the quotes.... it sounds awesome. What is it?????

'The compound return is the rate of return usually expressed as a percentage, that represents the cumulative effect that a series of gains or losses has on an original amount of capital over a period of time. Compound returns are usually expressed in annual terms, meaning that the percentage number that is reported represents the annualized rate at which capital has compounded over time. (thanks Google).

Basically, leaving your money invested (and reinvested) in something with a good return can stack your money up very, very quickly. Compound returns are often referred to as Compounded Interest Returns – this is essentially the same thing – except whenever you receive interest, you reinvest it back into your original investment.

Here are some charts to demonstrate just how powerful they are. It's amazing how much growth every % point can compound.

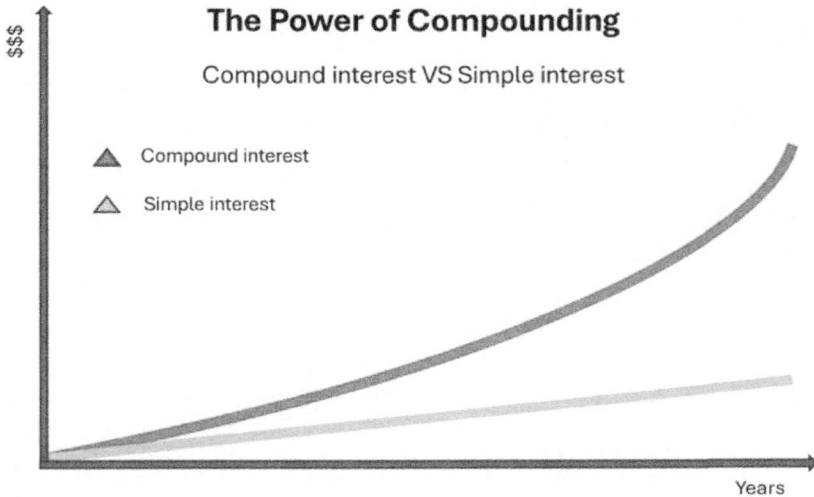

The Power of Compounding

Compound interest VS Simple interest

▲ Compound interest

△ Simple interest

$$$

Years

In the above chart, 'simple interest' essentially represents money-earning interest, but you never reinvest it. For example, you put $10000 into a fixed deposit with the bank at 5% interest. Each year, you will earn $500, and you just leave it sitting in the bank, or you will spend it. The 'compound interest' curve takes the $500 and reinvests it. The 'compound interest" curve demonstrates the power of patience.

The table below shows the rate of compounding returns on an initial investment of $1000 and how it compounds every year by reinvesting the gains (and how much of an impact every 1% makes to the compounding).

Note: On $10000, a 1% over 55 years = $7285 gains. That may not seem too much over 55 years (and I will cover this a little bit later), but why give that 1% to some financial adviser in management fees if it can be avoided without impacting your overall returns?

Note: 10% is the average return of the S&P500 over the last 100 years (it doesn't move in a straight line). That turns the $10000 at 10% into $1m around the 49-year mark. Thats impressive!

Note: 18% turns the $10000 at the 50-year mark to $39million. Yep, that is absolutely insane, BUT with the higher return comes VERY VERY HIGH RISK. This table becomes a good check and balance in that if you plan carefully, you don't need to take insane risks for pretty insane returns.

YEARS	1%	2%	4%	6%	8%
1	10,100	10,200	10,400	10,600	10,800
5	10,510	11,041	12,167	13,382	14,693
10	11,046	12,190	14,802	17,908	21,589
15	11,610	13,459	18,009	23,966	31,722
20	12,202	14,859	21,911	32,071	46,610
25	12,824	16,406	26,658	42,919	68,485
30	13,478	18,114	32,434	57,435	100,627
35	14,166	19,999	39,461	76,861	147,853
40	14,889	22,080	48,010	102,857	217,245
45	15,648	24,379	58,412	137,646	319,204
50	16,446	26,916	71,067	184,202	469,016
55	17,285	29,717	86,464	246,503	689,139

YEARS	10%	12%	14%	16%	18%
1	11,000	11,200	11,400	11,600	11,800
5	16,105	17,623	19,254	21,003	22,878
10	25,937	31,058	37,072	44,114	52,338
15	41,772	54,736	71,379	92,655	119,737
20	67,275	96,463	137,435	194,608	273,930
25	108,347	170,001	264,619	408,742	626,686
30	174,494	299,599	509,502	858,499	1,433,706
35	281,024	527,996	981,002	1,803,141	3,279,973
40	452,593	930,510	1,888,835	3,787,212	7,503,783
45	728,905	1,639,876	3,636,791	7,954,438	17,166,839
50	1,173,909	2,890,022	7,002,330	16,707,038	39,273,569
55	1,890,591	5,093,206	13,482,388	35,090,488	89,848,411

Can you see why I am in love with compounding returns and why I want to marry it??

Right, you have just feasted your eyes on compounding returns, but that's based on having an initial $10000 of your savings invested.

But what would happen if you could save another $10000 from your salary **every year**? Be prepared to be blown away!!!

In the next example below, at a 10% return, you hit $1m at the 25-year mark. WOW!

Note: This example stops the $10000 annual saving addition at the 40-year mark. Why? Well, at the 40-year mark at 10%, you have a net worth of $4.8million. Do you need more Financial Freedom? Then, keep on working.

Note: I recognise that in the early years, saving $ 10,000 per year may be a little tough, but this model also assumes you never surpass more than $ 10,000 per year in income saving.

Note: I trimmed this back to max 14% due to the table formatting (and if after 55 years of investing, you accumulated $109million and you still haven't found Financial Freedom, then either inflation has gone parabolic crazeee (or perhaps you have some extremely high spend patterns stashed away for the future). Trying to sustain a 14% return = HIGH RISK! Especially when you don't need to.

YEAR	+ Saving	1%	2%	4%	6%
1	10000	20,100	20,200	20,400	20,600
5	10000	61,520	63,081	66,330	69,753
10	10000	115,668	121,687	134,864	149,716
15	10000	172,579	186,393	218,245	256,725
20	10000	232,392	257,833	319,692	399,927
25	10000	295,256	336,709	443,117	591,564
30	10000	361,327	423,794	593,283	848,017
35	10000	430,769	519,944	775,983	1,191,209
40	10000	493,752	616,100	988,265	1,640,477
45		518,939	680,224	1,202,376	2,195,328
50		545,410	751,023	1,462,874	2,937,844
55		573,231	829,190	1,779,810	3,931,498

YEAR	+ Saving	8%	10%	12%	14%
1	10000	20,800	21,000	21,200	21,400
5	10000	73,359	77,156	81,152	85,355
10	10000	166,455	185,312	206,546	230,445
15	10000	303,243	359,497	427,533	509,804
20	10000	504,229	640,025	816,987	1,047,684
25	10000	799,544	1,091,818	1,503,339	2,083,327
30	10000	1,233,459	1,819,434	2,712,926	4,077,370
35	10000	1,871,021	2,991,268	4,844,631	7,916,729
40	10000	2,797,810	4,868,518	8,591,424	15,299,086
45		4,110,901	7,840,797	15,141,024	29,457,084
50		6,040,263	12,627,682	26,683,659	56,717,098
55		8,875,128	20,337,008	47,025,724	109,203,928

What I **strongly recommend** is that you play around with many of the free online compound calculators (or, even better, your own personalised spreadsheet (as below)) and keep using it to run all sorts of scenarios that fit your circumstances. It really helps to highlight the opportunity cost of spending versus saving versus investing. I use my spreadsheet quite regularly as I plug in my age, my net equity, and my current % return, and it roadmaps for me quite easily how my future $$ forecast is looking. It helps to drive home that I can be patient and not have to chase high-risk returns because even at 'market' return percentages, there will literally be 'cash to burn' when I am dead.

Below is a simple Excel spreadsheet you can easily create. You edit the yellow cells:

In this scenario, at age 23, you start with $5000 and maintain an 8% return while topping up each year with another $5000 of savings (until you hit 65). You hit $1m around 58 years old.

And check out the results if you make it to 100 years old. That's a great incentive to live a healthy balanced life – because that is some serious money you can gift away!

(Note I collapsed some of the rows to make it easier to present – but the actual spreadsheet has a separate row for each year.)

Age	Saving/Yr	1-Jan	Interest	Interest	31-Dec
23	**5000**		**8.0%**	400	5,400
24	5000	10,400	8.0%	832	11,232
25	5000	16,232	8.0%	1,299	17,531
26	5000	22,531	8.0%	1,802	24,333
27	5000	29,333	8.0%	2,347	31,680
28	5000	36,680	8.0%	2,934	39,614
29	5000	44,614	8.0%	3,569	48,183
30	5000	53,183	8.0%	4,255	57,438
35	5000	107,476	8.0%	8,598	116,075
40	5000	187,251	8.0%	14,980	202,231
45	5000	304,466	8.0%	24,357	328,824
50	5000	476,694	8.0%	38,136	514,830
55	5000	729,753	8.0%	58,380	788,133
56	5000	793,133	8.0%	63,451	856,584
57	5000	861,584	8.0%	68,927	930,511
58	5000	935,511	8.0%	74,841	**1,010,352**
59	5000	1,015,352	8.0%	81,228	1,096,580
60	5000	1,101,580	8.0%	88,126	1,189,706
61	5000	1,194,706	8.0%	95,576	1,290,283
62	5000	1,295,283	8.0%	103,623	1,398,905
63	5000	1,403,905	8.0%	112,312	1,516,218
64	5000	1,521,218	8.0%	121,697	1,642,915
65	5000	1,647,915	8.0%	131,833	1,779,748
66		1,779,748	8.0%	142,380	1,922,128
70		2,421,328	8.0%	193,706	2,615,034
75		3,557,725	8.0%	284,618	3,842,343
80		5,227,465	8.0%	418,197	5,645,662
85		7,680,861	8.0%	614,469	8,295,330
90		11,285,705	8.0%	902,856	12,188,562
95		16,582,403	8.0%	1,326,592	17,908,996
100		24,364,991	8.0%	1,949,199	26,314,190

And one more scenario... You are just starting and in your 1st year, you save $1000. But then each year, you increase that saving from your income by $1000. In this scenario, you hit $1m around 50 years old. This nicely illustrates how staying investment-focused equals good returns.

Age	Saving/Yr	1-Jan	Interest	Interest	31-Dec
23	1000	1,000	8.0%	80	1,080
24	2000	3,080	8.0%	246	3,326
25	3000	6,326	8.0%	506	6,833
26	4000	10,833	8.0%	867	11,699
27	5000	16,699	8.0%	1,336	18,035
28	6000	24,035	8.0%	1,923	25,958
29	7000	32,958	8.0%	2,637	35,594
30	8000	43,594	8.0%	3,488	47,082
35	13000	127,687	8.0%	10,215	137,901
40	18000	280,578	8.0%	22,446	303,025
45	23000	534,559	8.0%	42,765	577,324
50	28000	937,074	8.0%	74,966	1,012,040
51	29000	1,041,040	8.0%	83,283	1,124,323
52	30000	1,154,323	8.0%	92,346	1,246,669
53	31000	1,277,669	8.0%	102,214	1,379,883
54	32000	1,411,883	8.0%	112,951	1,524,833
55	33000	1,557,833	8.0%	124,627	1,682,460
60	38000	2,499,265	8.0%	199,941	2,699,206
65	43000	3,911,871	8.0%	312,950	4,224,820
70		5,747,821	8.0%	459,826	6,207,647
75		8,445,435	8.0%	675,635	9,121,070
80		12,409,115	8.0%	992,729	13,401,844
85		18,233,061	8.0%	1,458,645	19,691,706
90		26,790,349	8.0%	2,143,228	28,933,576
95		39,363,811	8.0%	3,149,105	42,512,916
100		57,838,353	8.0%	4,627,068	62,465,421

I have used 8% as that is a more reasonable number to base of given that you need to hold emergency cash and maybe some short-term investments (like bank fixed deposits),

And remember, just because the S&P has returned around 10% historically doesn't mean that's the future return. It's best to be conservative in your planning - that way, you don't feel too disappointed when things don't grow as fast as expected, but you also feel cool when you get a little upside you didn't plan for.

That's compounding returns. It's awesome!!

Note: Einstein lived between 1879 and 1955, and he knew about compounding returns, yet it's still hardly taught anywhere. I would rather have learnt about compounding returns than his famous E=MC2 (which I still don't really understand).

17. Understand the power of 2nd, 3rd, 4th, 5th.... income streams.

You work 1 job; you get 1 pay = active income.

You work 2 jobs; you get 2 pays = active income.

You work 3 jobs; you get 3 pays = active income.

But you only have a finite number of hours (24x7 = 168hours) you can work a week – and of course, the more hours you work, the less balanced lifestyle you are experiencing, and of course, you may end up being a bit shit at all jobs rather than really good at 1 job. Work as many jobs as you think you can manage but have a plan.

But the 2^{nd,} 3^{rd,} and 4th income streams don't need to involve working extra jobs – they just need you to allocate some of your 'downtime' to researching investment opportunities.

If you own a property and rent it out, Yippee, you have a 2nd income stream. As you have your money now working for you, then this is considered a 'Passive Income Stream."

Many company stocks (e.g. Coca-Cola/Microsoft), once owned, pay a stock dividend (typically 4 times per year). Dividends are considered a "Passive Income Stream."

The sooner you get your (saved) money working for you, the quicker you will create such passive income streams. Maybe it's better to spend a few hours a week planning how to make your money work for you rather than working a few hours a week to earn extra money - but you don't get it working for you?

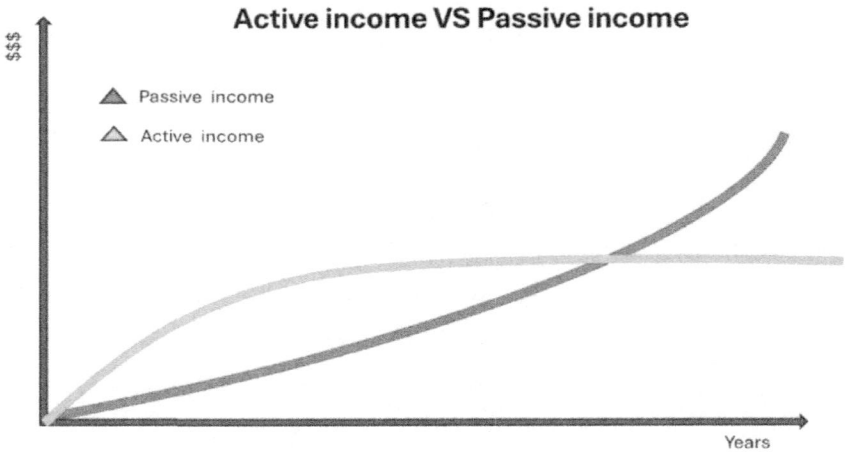

Active income VS Passive income

▲ Passive income

△ Active income

$$$

Years

There is a tipping point with Active versus Passive income. Once you have worked out how much annual income (or spending) you need for your Financial Freedom, you can put together a plan for when your passive income may exceed your required annual income. Passive income generally moves well with inflation, too. Property rents tend to go up over the long term, and company dividends tend to go up over the long term. I am quite big on breathing space, so I recommend making sure your passive income is quite a lot more than your annual spend – the more breathing space = less stress = less risk for the unforeseen.

Everyone will be different, but I essentially retired when my passive income was about 4 times greater than my budgeted spend per year (oh, and I also over-estimated my budgeted spend because I like to have breathing space in that, too). These days, my passive income easily exceeds my living expenses and my growth is typically quite a bit more than my last work salary, and as my passive income continues to grow (greater than inflation), I am confident I have got things covered.

Medical costs: As we get older, our medical costs will likely increase. I have a good medical insurance policy, BUT insurance policies are sneaky and have too much fine print that it's super difficult to know for sure what I may or may not be covered for. Am I covered 100%? I can't confirm this 100%, so in my retirement planning, I accept that one day, I may get hit with a big 'non-planned' medical expense. If it happens, I will be pissed off, but I am prepared for it, so I have managed the level of pissed off-ness. At some point (maybe 80?), my insurance policy may become way too expensive, so I will have some decisions to make - e.g. cancel the policy because I have only got 10 years to live and I have more than enough $$ to pay medical bills directly or relocate back to New Zealand because medical care is free. It's not a big concern now, but it is something I have on my radar for the future, and I will tighten up that plan along the way.

Breathing Space: In Thailand for a renewable yearly retirement visa (for foreigners) you need to maintain a minimum balance of 800,000 THB (approx. USD24k) in your personal Thai bank account. That's your money in your account so it is protected. Sometimes there is media talk that this might increase to 1,200,000 THB (approx. USD35k), and it's always interesting how many people start complaining on how this will really affect them, and they may need to consider retiring to another country in Asia (or return back to their home country). My key take away from this is that if you can't afford to allocate that extra US9k (in your personal bank account) then you may be retired but you haven't achieved Financial Freedom, or you haven't planned for any breathing space (or you are a negative person and just love complaining!).

18. Take advantage of investment tax benefits.

Many countries have some form of a tax benefit scheme, and they vary quite a lot by country, so take the time to understand what's available for your situation and make sure you take advantage of them. I personally don't qualify for any, so I can't give much advice on this other than to learn about them and decide how they may benefit you.

For example, the U.S. has a Roth IRA, which is an individual retirement account that you contribute to with after-tax dollars. While you don't get a tax break up front, your contributions and investment earnings grow tax-free.

New Zealand has Kiwisaver.

Australia has Super.

Singapore has CPF.

UK has ISA.

19. Assume no Government pension when you retire.

I'm not sure where you live and if your Government provides a pension when you retire, but from a Financial Freedom planning perspective - assume that by the time you retire, there will be NO pension. If your plan was based on their being one and then it gets changed (e.g. retirement age pushed back/pension amount reduced/you no longer qualify for it because you write with your left hand), then this can mess your plan up a bit. However, if you assume there isn't going to be one, and you retire, and there is one, then that's a cool little unplanned top-up.

With a global ageing population, I think it's going to be harder for Governments to retain pension levels over the coming decades. Australia has a means-tested pension system that basically says if your net wealth is above a certain threshold, then you don't qualify for a pension. I expect more countries may adopt this moving forward.

I get a little annoyed when I see someone saying on various social media channels, "It's not fair – you can't even live off the Government pension anymore." Note to the person moaning about this: I don't think Government pensions were ever designed to be 100% lived off – they were designed to provide you a little bit of a top-up later in life. You had about 30+ years to save for your retirement. Sorry, my book wasn't available back then.

Note that I reference Government pensions as opposed to work-related pensions. There are all sorts of different pension schemes available depending on your career. You will need to decide if this is a good way to contribute to funding your Financial Freedom plan or not. And make sure you understand the risk of that pension scheme defaulting, as there have been a few examples of this over the years. I only recall being offered one when I was about 20, but I figured I could get better returns by managing the money myself versus the company scheme. However, that was so long ago that I had no idea if I was correct or not. But then, I didn't stay with the same company/country, so it would not have worked for me anyway.

I don't receive and I don't qualify for any Government or company pension. I have no issue with that as they were NEVER part of my Financial Freedom plan.

20. Understand Good Debt versus Bad Debt!

Not all debt is equal!

- Debt can be good or bad—and part of that depends on how it's used.
- Generally, debt used to help build wealth or improve a person's financial situation is considered good debt.
- Generally, financial obligations that are unaffordable or don't offer long-term benefits might be considered bad debt.
- Any debt that might be considered good has the potential to become bad if it's not managed responsibly.

Hopefully, this section will be self-explanatory, but it's very important for moving forward. Here are the more common examples.

Credit card debt:

This is generally considered bad debt. You buy something you really really (really?) need but don't have the cash, so you put it on your credit card, and you don't pay it off within the month, and suddenly you are paying quite high interest rates for the thing you really really (really?) needed. Missed payments can go up to 20% interest rates = BIG OUCH!

If you really need it but don't have the cash to buy it, then consider buying something second-hand.

Maybe you shouldn't get a credit card; just get a debit card.

Here is a life challenge: Go through life without ever needing to put anything on the credit card that you don't pay off that month. This has worked for me, and it hasn't even been a challenge.

A new car:

A brand-new car looks cool and smells great and can really get those 'feel good neurons' working. What's not to love about buying a new car?

When you sign the papers and drive that car home, it still feels great, but by the time you have reached your home driveway, that new car has started to lose maybe 20%+ of its value – welcome to the world of depreciation. Wow, that was a very expensive drive home.

The opportunity cost of the new car versus an alternative investment looks something like the following: The average cost of a new vehicle in the U.S. is approximately $48,000 car, and they lose on average 20% depreciation over the first 1 year and a total of 40% over 5 years.

Year	Car Value	Depreciation		Investment 8.5%
0	$48,000	18%	$8,640	$48,000
1	$39,360	9%	$4,320	$52,080
2	$35,040	6%	$2,880	$56,160
3	$32,160	4%	$1,920	$60,240
4	$30,240	3%	$1,440	$64,320
5	$28,800			$68,400
Gain/Loss	-$19,200	-40%	$19,200	$20,400

The above assumes NO loan repayments on the initial $48,000.

The opportunity cost on the $48,000 if it was earning 8.5% interest instead is $20,400. Note this is NOT compounded/reinvested. It's just earning $4080 each year (48000 x 8.5% = 4080).

4080 x 5 years = 20400.

So, depreciation of $19200 + potential investment of $20,400 = an opportunity cost of $39600 over 5 years.

Imagine what those numbers would look like if you were also paying off debt when you bought that new car. Buying a new car with a loan = extra bad debt!!

What about a used car? You can get a good car that still works very well, but its speed of depreciation has slowed down a lot.

Buying a used car with a loan = maybe bad debt/or maybe good debt? If that car is fit for purpose value-wise and enables you to get to work to earn income, then maybe it's a good debt!

Buying a car? Crunch the numbers in a spreadsheet and listen to the numbers and not your emotions.

I have never owned a new car and don't think I ever will buy one. When I left high school, I needed a car, so I bought an old boring brown car – my friends took the piss out of me cause it was very uncool looking – but in the days when drinking and driving was a little borderline (Yep, it was illegal but only if you got caught) it was great driving what looked like grandmas car – I never got pulled over.

I have had a few second-hand cars over the years, but they are typically about 5 years old. Cars are NOT my thing. These days, I own a 125cc scooter. Costs me about USD3/week to fill it up = easy!

Oh, and if I was ever gifted a fast red sports car – I would sell it immediately because who wants to look 'Super Cringey'?

Property debt (also known as a mortgage):

Refer to the ROI (Return on Investment section) and the Property section further down, but if you do your due diligence correctly, then having a mortgage can be a very good debt.

If it's a property you rent out for passive income, then so long as once rented out and all expenses are taken into consideration (including the mortgage repayments), you have positive cash flow, then this is presented as GOOD DEBT.

If it's the property you live in, but after taking in all the related expenses (including the mortgage repayments), the total costs are less than or not too far from what you would pay in rent, then this is presented as GOOD DEBT.

Plus, you get the advantage over time of the property going up in value.

In summary, when it comes to Bad Debt versus Good Debt, it's important to do your due diligence and make decisions based on numbers - not emotion. If not sure, go back and read "Kiss Your Ego Goodbye" and "Consumerism - Needs vs Wants," as they can easily lead you down the dark path of bad debt!

Coming up next is a very interesting and, some may say, controversial form of debt. Let's roll up our sleeves and get ready to Muay Thai!!

21. Is a University degree good debt or bad debt??

This is likely to vary by country, but after doing some quick searches of a few countries, Google indicates that student University debt averages can range from USD20k to USD40k+ easily enough. Ouch, as that's a large amount of money to pay back at such a young age.

Is it good debt or bad debt? Well, that is going to depend on you!

My recommendation is to use your Excel brain and calculate the ROI on those returns before committing to University.

- If you start University but don't finish it, then there is a high chance that you will be left with bad debt.
- If you complete University but then get a job in a totally different field than what your degree was based on, then there is a chance that you will be left with bad debt.
- If you complete your degree, then add a second degree (or a PhD), and it doesn't get you much up the $$$ ladder, then there is a chance that you have added some bad debt.
- If you complete your degree and it gets you a job well up the $$$ ladder, then there is a high chance this is good debt.

I have friends who went to University, and it worked out very well for them.

I have friends who went to University, and it didn't seem to make much difference in their careers.

I have friends who didn't go to University, and it worked out well for them.

The recurring pattern is that it comes down to the individual and how they apply themselves to University and the workforce in general.

As mentioned above, I never went to University. Turned out it is something I am very pleased about. I started work in 1986 at 18 as a computer trainee for a plastic bag manufacturer in my local city (population 100k people). I had zero experience as we didn't even have computers at our school. I chose this job because there was the revolutionary saying, "One day, there will be computers on every desk." I was embracing the technology of the future... (Yep, weird when I look back at it). I worked with them for 4 years before heading to the UK. I was quickly promoted to a systems administrator and then quickly promoted to a systems supervisor. When I left for the UK at the age of 22, I had no debt and actually had a decent amount of my salary saved. In comparison, some of my friends were just finishing University, and they had some University debt (University debt probably wasn't as bad back in the late 80s as almost everyone did part-time/holiday work), but their starting salary was less than what I was earning as I had the advantage of 4years actual work experience.

So, I could get my money working for me a little bit earlier than others (if only someone had taught me, "Shit no one teaches us" back then. Arrrgghhh!!

There isn't a Yes or No answer here – simply run the numbers and make the most of the opportunities that get presented to you.

But what career should I pursue?

22. Career Choice: Chase your passion or chase the money ladder.

No easy answer here? Or maybe there is!

If you don't have something you are passionate about, then chase the money ladder! Simple. Next topic!

OK, let me expand on this.

Some people I consider super lucky because they have something they are really passionate about, and they just love doing it. If you are one of these people, then that's awesome, and you should chase your passion. It still requires hard and smart work, planning, and all the other stuff that will get you to your Financial Freedom. Applying yourself to something you are passionate about will typically bring you a wide range of personal rewards. And maybe you get to your Financial Freedom goal, and you just keep going = awesome.

Meanwhile, the other 80 to 90% per cent of us have no idea what we are career-wise passionate about, and we bumble through high school (even though we may have great grades) and still can't answer that tricky question: What do you want to be when you grow up?

This is where some go to University, and time passes (with debt), and they still are none the wiser after 4 years.

This is where many of us take the first job that kinda comes our way, and we get the initial buzz that we got a job, but that buzz fades quite quickly.

If you don't know what you really want to do, then in true capitalist style, chase the money ladder because you have mainly 2 scenarios that can play out:

1: I did a job I wasn't overly passionate about, and the money was kind of shit.

2: I did a job I wasn't overly passionate about, and the money was pretty good.

Option 1: you are probably going to do that job for a lot longer than Option 2.

Option 2 gives you a faster roadmap potential to Financial Freedom.

And anyone who says, "But money can't buy you happiness," is a very narrow thinker. What money can buy you is OPTIONS. In scenario 2, that OPTION is to finish your career earlier because you have more money, and you could get that money working for you to build a 2nd and 3rd and 4th passive income.

I will cover career hacks later that really helped me, and I hope they can help you, but before that, here is a little side rant and here's a couple of key tips:

Side Rant: I hope it has improved, but from my experience, schools were bad at helping us decide what career options suited us at an individual level. We had a career/counsellor adviser, but I don't recall ever having a one-on-one session with him. My parents were shit at it too.

I got super pissed off with my dad, who basically farmed my 6 older brothers out of the house by 16 or 17 to join the army or police or navy or prison service. He knew I never wanted to do any of them, and then one day, when I was about 16, he did the old "Hey, you should join the army sales pitch as it will be really good for you" Shit it pissed me off because at no time did he ever try to understand ME!

I ended up working in the tech industry, but I was never a tech geek. My strength was mainly operational efficiency. I will expand on this much later. I was fortunately pretty focussed workwise and I never held the same role for > 2 years, which was cool because although I was never passionate about my career. I have always enjoyed the new challenges I faced. If I had moments when I would think, "Oh, this work thing is a bit shit," it never really bothered me because I would remind myself I am partly working for this company, but I am mainly working to get more money to make my money work for me.

Key tip: Try to avoid taking on a job that you can learn in a day, a week, a month, or even a year. That, by default, likely has very limited growth capacity (and boring too!)

Limited personal growth capacity = limited income growth capacity.

23. Will your career be relevant (in demand) in 5, 10, 15 or 20 years?

OK, the above needs its own mini-chapter (and probably a book). With all the buzz around AI, it's probably more relevant than ever, so it's an important time to ask this question.

Google (in fact, you can even ask AI itself) has a lot of content on what jobs will likely go and what jobs will phase out at some point, thanks to AI. Before deciding on your career, ask AI if they are going to steal it from you and, if so, when. Or even better, ask AI how you can work as a team to enable you to thrive in your career.

If, like me, you are quite uncreative then AI, if known how to team up together, can be a great friend indeed. (the reality is that AI isn't going away - so buddy up with it and unleash your potential).

Fortunately, there are some cool tools that will always be in demand, such as good common sense, good communication skills, leadership skills, work integrity, working hard and smart, and many more.

If you are just starting out, then think about the career path ahead of you and how to make it work best for you. If you are already in a career that you enjoy, then spend some time AI'ing how to ensure you stay relevant to that career.

This also ties into how to differentiate yourself, but I will put this at the end of the book as it works well with some suggested career hacks, so more on this later.

24. Invest in things you understand and are interested in.

I will cover later what sort of things have a good historic track record for investing in, but a good tip is to invest in things you are interested in. If you are interested in it, then you are more likely to do good due diligence on the opportunity and keep track of it.

I had someone approach me once about some investment opportunity involving tractors. Yep, weird! I asked a few questions (based on my Excel brain) and quickly assessed that I didn't understand it and that tractors just weren't my thing. Therefore, I didn't bother to pursue the opportunity any further.

I had someone approach me once about some investment opportunity involving wine barrels in Scotland. A little less weird! I asked a few questions (based on my Excel brain) and quickly assessed that I didn't understand it and wine barrels just aren't my thing. Therefore, I didn't bother to pursue the opportunity any further.

Property investments have always interested me, and I have made a few of these over the years.

Stock/ETF investments over the past 10 years have interested me more, and I am actively engaged in long-term (not day trading) investing.

Crypto. I have spent time reviewing, but for me personally, it's got too many unanswered questions, so it's not my thing. I tend not to follow it in much detail because I don't fully understand it or am not interested in it.

Technology: I quite like keeping pace with the future of technology. Not at a tech geek level but more at a social impact level, for example:

- When electric robotaxis and self-driving become the norm, how many jobs will be 100% disrupted? Do we need traffic lights? Do we need to own a car or a second car? In Asia, where not everyone has ready access to charge points, can everyone really go electric (without a standard-sized swap-out battery)?
- When laboratory stem cell meat is cheaper than buying chicken at the supermarket, will it be widely embraced? What happens to the farmland – does it all become national parks? What is the future for farmers? What is the future for cows and sheep? Will vegetarians eat stem cell meat?
- When vertical farming in cities becomes more effective than vegetable farming in the countryside, then will that farmland go back to national parks? What is the future for farmers? If you can grow a mango in Toronto, then does that kill the mango industry in Thailand?
- When vertical take-off vehicles (drones that can carry humans) are the norm, then do we still need electric cars and robotaxis?
- When we have semiconductor chips inserted into our forearms, then will we even care about the transgender sports debate because we will now be focused on the javelin thrower with an Nvidia chip; who beat the javelin thrower with an Intel chip?

I sidetracked a bit on the Technology topic. It is stuff that I am quite interested in and like to follow, but I don't invest in it for just those reasons alone. My stock/ETF portfolio has a solid broad technology focus because I believe it is one sector of the industry that will never go away. I also invest (speculate) a little in potentially next-breakthrough technologies, but it's a very small part of my portfolio.

25. Balance your portfolio.

Once you start to build out your investment portfolio, you need to ensure you are aware of the need to have a balanced portfolio. This is essentially reducing the risk of having all the eggs in one basket. Or in other words – one investment shits itself, but not all. A good example: I think Microsoft, the company, and the stock is a fairly reliable long-term stock investment, and I hold some Microsoft stock, BUT I ensure it never becomes >5% of my total stock portfolio. Imagine it was 100%, and then suddenly they go bankrupt: I don't need to take all that risk when I just need to keep my portfolio balanced and Microsoft around 5%.

This can get a little tricky to navigate as it does have a few variances to consider:

Your three main criteria for investing are generally as follows:

- How much $$$ do I want to allocate for emergencies (e.g., if I lose my job):
- How much $$$ do I want to allocate for a short-term goal (e.g. I want to put a deposit on a property, so as I save for that deposit, it might take me 5 years, and I want to safeguard that money).
- How much $$$ do I want to allocate in the long term? (15 years plus).
- There is a 4^{th,} and that is how much I want to speculate with for that super high get RXXX return. I don't recommend this one until at least the above 3 are balanced and sorted out. High risk, high reward greed-fuelled trap.

When you are just starting out, you likely will not have a large amount of $$$ for investing, so your first few years may not be much of a balanced portfolio – but that's OK – because you have a draft plan on what your portfolio may look like in year 2 and year 5 and year 10+.

71

As people get older, it is typically recommended that they increase their portfolio with things such as fixed-term deposits (with the bank) and/or bonds and or stocks/ETFs paying dividends. I think sometimes this will also depend on how much breathing space you have when you retire. For example, I don't bother with bonds (more about these later), but I do ensure I maintain a decent dividend focus in my portfolio. Over the next 15+ years, these dividends should continue to grow, so by the time I am in my 70s, I expect my passive income from dividends will be very good.

Your Financial Freedom roadmap should ideally start and finish with something nicely balanced.

26. Read lots, but not everything you read is gospel.

There is so much content out there, as mentioned earlier, such as YouTube, Instagram, blogs, financial forums, etc., and a lot of books written by some very successful investors. A couple of famous investors who have books and are quoted regularly are people like Warren Buffet and Peter Lynch. I like reading (it used to be my safe space as a kid), and I read about 18 books per year, mostly Non-Fiction, but when it comes to investment-related books, I don't take it as 100% must-do. I kinda work out what works for me and will adapt things to my style. And this includes what's in this book. I doubt if anyone would want to (and I wouldn't overly recommend it) apply my approach exactly to their approach (this will become clearer on the 'tight arse' later.

I haven't embraced listening to podcasts much; it's just not really my thing (maybe when my eyes stop working). I have also become a bit of a skim reader these days – probably due to reading e-books, and I find that a lot of author content just goes overly detailed for me. I recently read a book on outer space physics: Yep, I got the concept and have learnt a lot, but I don't need to know all the details of a "Doppler Shift."

27: Talk 'investing' with others: It doesn't have to be Taboo!!

As a kid, my parents never talked about money or investing. I have no idea what they invested in.

As a kid, my teachers never talked about money or investing. I have no idea what they invested in.

I have 6 older brothers, but I have never discussed investment stuff with them.

With my friends growing up = nope, never discussed.

It wasn't until I was about 29 that I started living in Hong Kong. We would play rugby on Saturday, and on Sunday, we would often chill at the beach at Repulse Bay. The conversation would typically talk about the game we played yesterday, then the dumb stuff we got up to that evening and then weirdly, it would turn to someone saying, "Hey, I've been looking into this thingy as a possible investment - ever heard of it? what do you think?" This is my first real memory of talking about investing with anyone!! Wow – 29. Why so late in life???

The cool thing about talking about investing is it keeps your mind in the game; it hopefully becomes something that is easier to understand and become interested in, and it helps you find the lane that best works for you.

It doesn't have to involve telling anyone how much money you have or learning about how much money they have. I have held Financial Freedom sessions at my place, and not once has anyone been asked to (nor have they told me) how much money they earn or have – it's not required. I have no idea how much money any of my friends or family have, and I don't care. And the only person who knows how much money I have is me. People can find out when I am dead, I guess!!

So don't make it a taboo topic – talk about it openly as a great way to sound-board stuff and come up with ideas/opportunities that work for you. And if someone is trying to pry how much money you have. (or trying to show-off with what they **MAY** have), then just tell them that you are quoting a very nice but very direct Kiwi author when you tell them to 'budgie off'!

28. Be a saver - not a spender.

Pretty obvious, but achieving Financial Freedom earlier is best achieved by being a saver. If you are a spender and don't want to change those habits, then plan on your Financial Freedom taking much longer.

However, if you are a spender, I recommend you take the time to assess the things you are spending your money on that may not be needed or rewarding for you. Later I present a simple spreadsheet to track your income versus your spending, and this becomes a good little tool to highlight what things you could easily cut back on just to give you a little more savings for investing. It may also highlight the things that may not be easy to cut back on, but they can make a big difference in more savings. Yet again, getting the details in a spreadsheet helps remove the emotion. This all ties back into ego and consumerism and, of course, finding the balance that works best for you.

But spending without taking the time to acknowledge and accept it is a bit like an addiction. I have had many experiences with people who are adamant they are savers, and there is **no way** they could cut back on their spending patterns, and when they start to reveal the details of what they spend, then to me, it seems quite easy to change. Some examples:

Singapore friend spending $SGD4/day on his coffee fix. Wayne spending $SGD1/day at the local hawker centre on his equivalent coffee fix (teh ping – iced tea). (SGD1000/year difference = USD750). More on this opportunity cost later when I present the 'Coffee Fix' formula to you.

A couple from Europe are living in Singapore on very good salaries but are struggling to save money because Singapore is so expensive. It was a married couple with no kids renting a 4-bedroom landed property. Hmmmm, couldn't think of any way to cut back on their spending?

A friend is buying a brand-new car in Singapore. Singapore is the most expensive country in the world for buying and owning a car. He was single. It would've been significantly cheaper to have taxied everywhere.

Someone I know would upgrade to premium class on a flight - but the flight was only 90 minutes long – but would complain about how expensive Singapore was??

A friend treats herself to another USD100 dinner because she got a free USD100 dinner gift voucher – so her dinner really only cost USD50. Waynes thought process is you saved USD100 on a great dinner– why not just stick with that!

Wayne gets a promotion at work, and a colleague says, "Wayne, you will need to buy a car now to help improve your image." Waynes's response "Nah, I will still cycle to and from work."

And many, many more...

\Why am I a saver? Mum was very tight with money. I went to school with jam sandwiches when many other kids had ham and cheese sandwiches. My oldest brother is 13 years older than me, and my school uniform often had his name inked into it, so a lot of my clothes were 10 to 13 years old. But my best memory was when I was about 13, and I bought a 1.5l of coke home from the corner shop with some pocket money I found(?), and my mum severely scolds me "why waste money on that when we have cordial in the fridge?" Fortunately, by 13, I was taller than Mum, so it was a verbal beating as opposed to the physical 'clip across the ears' she used to hand out (different times, I guess). Did these childhood experiences make me a saver? Who knows!

Worst day of my early childhood life: in New Zealand, if you wanted milk (like many countries back then), you put the empty glass milk bottles outside with the coins in the bottles and the milkman would take the bottles and the coins and replace with full bottles of milk. Some evenings, me (about aged 5) and my older brother (about aged 7) used to go walkies a few kms from our place and steal the milk bottle money. Milk was about 3 cents a bottle, so on a good evening, we could easily make about 30 cents each. It was our super-secret, although we suspected Mum knew about it. What was the worst day of my childhood? They replaced coins with pre-paid (non-transferable) plastic tokens, and that was the end of our cash business (for at least a few weeks). Looking back, were we opportunists or entrepreneurs or just little shits? Yep, OK, we were little shits! But we grew up to be very honest people (eventually)!

29. Don't be too much of a Tight Arse.

I am a bit of a tight arse – I don't really like spending money, and so it's actually very rare for me to treat myself by spending money on myself – I tend to just purchase what I think is 'good enough.' This probably has gotten a little worse since I have gotten older as I embrace the minimalist approach more. It is something I need to find a better balance with, especially as it's not the best trait when you have a partner.

I also don't like people spending money on me, as it makes me feel a little uncomfortable and awkward.

At work, I used to remind staff as we budgeted things not to confuse a cost-conscious mindset with being cheap. We don't always listen to our own advice, I guess.

The key takeaway is to make sure you find the right balance that works for you, but also make sure that balance enables you to stay on target for your Financial Freedom plan.

ME	$$$
NOT ME	$$$$$$$$$$$$$$$$$$$$$$$$$$$$$$$$$$$$$
YOU	???????????

If you were suddenly awarded USD 10 million what would you spend it on? My answer = probably a new mountain bike.

30. Never loan money to friends/family WITHOUT a loan agreement with penalties.

This one may be a little bit difficult to stick to as it will depend very much on your family and friends and especially your societal culture. But here's the practical side to this statement:

For Financial Freedom planning, it's important to ensure your money is working for you. That's hard to achieve when your money is (maybe??) working for someone else. Also, a serious question needs to be asked: Are you simply feeding a friend/family members really bad habit (gambling/credit card debt/ ego, etc.)? I think the following can, unfortunately, be a little too common:

"Hey, best buddy lend me some money, please – I am really in the shit. I will pay you back – I promise."

6 months later...

"Hey, best buddy lend me some money, please – I am really in the shit. I will pay you back – I promise."

6 months later...

"Hey, best buddy lend me some money, please – I am really in the shit. I will pay you back – I promise."

What to do? My advice/experience is as follows:

Fortunately, I haven't been asked too many times to lend people money. Maybe they think I don't have any? Maybe they know I am a tight arse? Maybe they know I will not 'gift' money?

However, when asked, I ensure I fully understand why the money is needed and assess their ability and intent to pay it back. I also make them feel guilty/shit/stink for asking me (or anyone). Remember, these aren't strangers, I know them quite well, which also forms part of my assessment process.

In a few cases, I have simply refused to lend the money because it's been their bad habit, or they have no plan or roadmap on how to pay the loan back.

When I have agreed to lend the money, I create a very simple loan agreement (I use a template taken from the internet), and I write out the loan terms. i.e. you agree to borrow $$XXX, and you agree to repay this $$XXX in 5 equal instalments over the next 5 months. During this period, I will charge you zero interest; however, in the event of default of repayment, you will be charged 2% interest per month" (or something similar to above).

If the friend/family member says, "Yes, that is no problem. Thanks very much. I really appreciate this: it's going to be a huge help, and I won't ask again". Then those are positive signs, which is great.

If the friend/family member says, "I am trying to exploit their situation, and I have no trust in them. I am worse than a loan shark", then I withdraw the loan offer and politely tell them to go back to the bank(s) and ask them again. I have done this twice.

When I have loaned money, it has always been paid back on schedule. No one has defaulted on me!

Why is my approach important (regardless of how close this person is to me and even if the money they want to borrow is a relatively small amount)? The reality is I am doing this person a huge favour by ensuring they take responsibility and accountability for their actions that got them into this spot in the first place. We can consider it Tough Love!

31. Have a Will and understand your inheritance tax.

While we are on the yukky topic of legal agreements, I will quickly throw this one into the mix.

Make 2 Wills as follows:

1: A living Will: you are in a vegetative state in a hospital, and a loved one needs to approve the pulling of the plug so you can die. This one is simple: it's designed to reduce any guilt your loved one may feel for coming to such a decision (along with the physician). Reduces the burden so much more when they can say to themselves and others, "This is what Wayne wanted," as opposed to "Maybe, kind of, I don't know for sure what Wayne wanted"

2: An inheritance Will: What happens when you are dead to all your assets? Simple reason: we typically never know when we are going to die, and this takes the burden of those left behind trying to work out (and maybe even fight) what to do with the assets. Even if the legal default is, the assets go to Mum and Dad (it is great to spell it out clearly so some sneaky aunty doesn't try to interfere in the process).

Both of these have quite a few document templates that can be easily found online, and you don't need a 3rd party lawyer to make it legal (double-check this for your country). The good thing about having these documents done yourself is you can amend them along the way again without incurring legal costs, and it gives you some peace of mind.

Inheritance tax: Some countries have some Government rules around inheritance tax.

UK for anything above STG350k can = % inheritance tax

Australia and New Zealand = 0% inheritance tax.

Something to factor into and plan as you get older.

An odd event I read about recently. A foreigner died in Asia, and there was a 'fund' to assist with the cost of sending the coffin back to Europe. My common sense brain immediately thought it would be better to have the body cremated in Asia as it's a lot cheaper to send back the ashes. I didn't make a spreadsheet for this though!

But this does lead nicely to the next guideline.

32. Insurances – cover yourself.

They are ugly things and often very grey on what is/isn't covered, but it's not worth the financial risk of avoiding them. Make sure you have got them covered (and they cover you to a point where you feel comfortable). They can include (but not limited to):

Medical
Travel
Property
House Content
Vehicle
Pet
....and I am sure there are a few others.

Sometimes, in Thailand, a European tourist who gets hospitalised (typically a motorcycle accident) gets hit with a big medical bill, and they don't have any travel insurance, so they launch a GoFundMe.

Hmmm, you can afford a trip overseas all the way from Europe, but you can't afford the extra $100 for travel insurance?

33. Is having children good for your Financial Freedom plan?

Definitely not! Next topic...

No doubt about it, but kids can be expensive, but then the reason for having kids should simply tie into "I want kid(s) because I really want kid(s). Just make sure you take the time to understand the potential financial costs of having a kid(s). Yep, put it in a spreadsheet. It is better to have a range of potential costs and a budget for it than "Shit, I had no idea a 4-year-old **needed** an iPhone, a MacBook and an iPad."

From a Financial Freedom planning perspective, I don't overly recommend saving money for your kids later in life. I have met a few people who want to buy their kid their first property, which is very admirable but probably not worth the cost of giving up 5++ years of your own earlier Financial Freedom.

I think a cooler thing to do for your kids' financial well-being is to raise them with some of the points covered in this book, for example, openly talk to your kids about financial stuff, manage their spending habits by leading by example.

I have done a couple of rounds of the kitchen table sessions, and the teenagers have walked away and thanked me, saying, "That's awesome, we learnt so much," and the parents have said, "That's pretty much what we have been telling them, but they don't seem to listen." My feedback to the parent has been, "Well, of course, they won't listen to you – they are teenagers, and you are the parents," and I have also jokingly advised the parents that maybe using the word 'shit' a lot will help.

If I had kids on the day they were born, I would invest a small amount in the S&P500 index tracking ETF (more on that ETF later), and then, every birthday, invest a little bit more. At the right age (maybe 8), I would let them know what I am doing and start to engage them in the process. At the age of 20, they can now manage this directly but only on the agreement that they NEVER sell it without mum and dad being part of the review process (forming long-term financial trust at a very early age, I think, is very cool).

On the flip side, don't expect your kids to finance you in retirement. That's not cool, as you remove the opportunity for your young adult kids to get ahead of the bunch. Remember, being able to get your money working for you in your 20s is a real leg up in life. Bit of a speed bump when some of the money is not working for the kid but is being used to support mum and dad. I recognise this is more difficult to follow in many countries. In Thailand, this is not so easy to implement in the current 50+-year-old generation, but hopefully, the newer generations coming through can find a better way to be more self-supporting in their older age.

Why don't I have kids? "Because I am a very, very bad man"! That's what I was told by a lady about 60 years old, along with her friends, when I was backpacking Turkmenistan about 6 years ago.

"What about your family name? It's important to keep your family name going" That is what I was told by a Chinese lady in China about 6 years ago. I didn't ask her what her last name was, but I was pretty sure it would've been one of the most common surnames in the world.

These days, when I get challenged for not having kids, I just piss-take the following response to them: "Because I am an environmentalist."

OK, why don't I have kids? Never had a paternal calling to want kids – as simple as that. Who knows what influence my growing up in a big family may or may not have had – and given I will never know, then no point analysing it. If I had kids, I guess I would've worked until they had at least left high school and/or University.

Here's an interesting scenario:

Sometimes parents send their kids to private schools even though there are public schools in their area. Rather than debate the pros and cons of this and the associated cost of it, let's assume this scenario (oh, I wish it was me – too bad my school was free)!

Wayne (aged 12): Hey folks so you are going to send me to that private high school for the next 5 years and at $20k/year that will cost $100k?

Folks: Yes, that's correct.

Wayne: How about instead I go to the local free school. I promise I will study really hard, make sure I pass my exams and at the end you will reward me with $95k (which I will then invest hopefully in a property deposit). Do we have a deal???

34. Plan as a couple.

OK, I have now moved on from giving parental advice to giving marital advice (something I am also poorly qualified for).

You and your partner are starting your financial journey together = that's awesome as the power of 2 is better than the power of 1, so you should be able to move forward financially quicker, BUT it's important to be very transparent with each other and agree on the general framework of what happens if the relationship fails: protecting each other before it turns bad is GOOD LOVE.

Hard to get very clear divorce rates from online (and it varies a bit by country), but generally, for many countries, the chance of divorce is 50%+. You could put that into a spreadsheet before making a decision on marriage or not, but then that is being way too much of a spreadsheet nerd!

Also note many countries have 'de facto' laws, which means, for example, if you are living in the same house as a couple (not married) for say, 12 months, then there are legal implications if you split up on items such as property and other financial assets. It is best to do your homework based on where you live up front and have an agreed (signed?) plan before things turn to shit (which hopefully they won't).

35. Stay away from negative people!

This is relevant to everything in life, not just investing for Financial Freedom, but nothing worse than sound-boarding an idea or opportunity with someone who's negative.

It's great to sound-board an idea or opportunity to someone who may not agree with you as there is a lot to be learnt from that, but the narrative should be designed in a positive, supportive manner, such as "Hey, sounds really interesting. Have you thought of this? How does that work? How does that fit into the bigger picture, etc." "Constructive feedback" I believe it is called!

Versus "that's such a stupid idea - no way that will ever work – you're too lazy – you're heads in the clouds - you're dreaming."

"Being a tosser" I believe it is called!

I moved around a bit as a kid (Dad was in the army) but was fortunate to pretty much start and finish at the same high school. When in high school, you tend to gravitate to the kids you get on with, and you don't over-analyse behaviour patterns too much. I then left school and went straight to work and had work colleague friends (you can't choose your work colleagues when just starting out). I also played rugby for the local club, so I had rugby friends. Plus, I have a large family. I was lucky cause I didn't really have negative people in my life, so it didn't overly influence me. But I think around the age of 25, I decided I was going to ensure I keep away from negative people. No specific name springs to mind - but I still maintain this thought process today. I meet the odd negative person, and I still make sure I don't give them much of my time (or very occasionally, I may wind them up – it's easy to push their buttons). So, a cool Financial Freedom and life lesson is to avoid negative people. If you can't 100% avoid them (maybe it's your mum or your grandad, "Ohh, when we were young"), then find a way that you can manage it (most likely by laughing at it), but don't let it hold you back. Wasted energy!

Similarly, it's great to have positive role models/mentors in life. I don't really have any specific name that jumps out at me, but what I learned early on is that you can take negative role models, and they can also teach you a lot. "No way am I going to be like them" can be just as powerful.

36. Don't play the victim.

And so, the point above plays nicely into this one. When it comes to Financial Freedom, you may find that the challenge ahead of you is much harder than most (including those around you). Yep, that sucks big time, BUT it's pretty cool as well because when you break through those things that could hold you back, it makes it even cooler and more rewarding. If you play the victim, it will certainly hold you back and just makes life, in general, a bit more shit.

I am super grateful I was born in New Zealand (that's just luck), as it gave me access to free education (and fun outdoors stuff).

When I was about 14, I thought I would go to University and be a lawyer. I'm not sure what kind, but I thought I could manage a debate, and the money would be awesome. Anyway, by the time I got to 17, my home life was really shit, and the University option was not going to work for me as I didn't want to be dependent at all on my father (mum had recently died/dad suddenly remarried within 3 months/we didn't really ever get on), so I basically went and got a job at 18 and just got on with life. I could play a victim card here, maybe. "I didn't go to University, booo hoooo, it's not fair," but it never crossed my mind! Yep, my level of 'potential victim' may be very minuscule to your own experience – but regardless, playing victim gets you nowhere.

Oh, and you know what's cool? From the week after I left school at 18, I was totally independent, so I pretty much achieved my Financial Freedom all by myself – that makes it even cooler than just cool when I look back on it.

37. Self-motivation is key.

Like most things in life – moving forward is mainly dependent on yourself. As covered earlier, writing down your goals helps keep you focused, and that equates to motivation as well. Don't rely on others to keep pushing you and pushing you because, eventually, you will just want to bitch slap them. Struggling with self-motivation? This is where talking to other like-minded people may help or break a big task down into lots of smaller tasks.

I had the idea to write this book about 4 years ago, but it's been a really slow process for me. I wrote it down in my goal for 2021 and drafted the main headings, then did nothing with it. Then it was in my 2022 goal list, and I worked on it a little bit more and then in my 2023 goal list, and I was getting pissed at myself for not getting on with it. Then I started telling people I had started to write this book because I knew once I told people I would do it, then it created a little extra pressure on myself to just get on with it. In July 2024, I have started writing this chapter. Let's see if I have the self-motivation to complete it by this year.

A very accurate lesson in life is, "If you want something done, then give it to a busy person." I am not a very busy person these days, so I think that makes me a bit lazy.

I read somewhere that the simple habit of making your bed in the morning is a really positive way to start the day and helps to keep you focused and disciplined as you go about things. If I didn't make my bed as a kid, I would get a smack – even though there is no one to smack me anymore, I still make my bed 1st thing in the morning (even if I am staying in a hotel).

Another simple habit is 'try really hard not to be late.' You lose a lot of credibility if you become the 'they are always late person'.

38. Don't limit goals to just financial goals.

OK, don't play the victim/stay away from negative people/self-motivation is key: what next? I start giving you dietary advice and want to be the world's best life coach. No (not exactly), but here's something that is hopefully really interesting:

If you get into the habit of tracking your financial goals and their progress, it actually becomes really easy to throw in a few non-financial goals too. Again, writing them down makes it more likely you will achieve them. When I sit down at my spreadsheet in December to figure out my financial goals for the coming year, I always add some non-financial goals too. In addition to wealth, I include health/fitness/experience/education.

Here are my typical other goals:

Stay < 80kgs. For as long as I can remember, I have ranged between 78 and 80 kgs. Sometimes, I might slip to about 77kgs, but I never slip up to 81kgs. It's been a long-term goal of mine, and it has, by default, become a life goal. Around 78kgs is a good weight for me to keep fit and have the energy to achieve my exercise lifestyle. If I get a bit sick/injured for a few weeks and can't exercise, then I automatically cut down on my sugar treats – a simple natural trade-off.

Do 2 fitness endurance events. This varies a bit, but for 2024, I have done a 100km self-supported walk (17.39 hours), and I walked 20kms carrying 20kgs. These weren't specifically written down in my January plan – but I know I need to come up with at least 2 during the year. I like the challenge, but it also fits in nicely with my keeping fitness/exercise as part of my natural way of life.

Do 3 travel adventures. For 2024 I have done the full length of Sumatra/Indonesia, including a 1600km north loop on a 125cc rental scooter and I did Xining/China to Delhi/India overland (through Tibet) on public transport. I will need to roll one adventure over to 2025.

Read 16 books per year. I complete that one easily.

Become more patient – difficult to measure, but I think over the year(s), I keep improving. A few years ago, I had "become a better listener" and "learn to show empathy" (which is not natural for me), and I feel I have improved on them quite well.

Improve my Thai – this is my brick wall. I struggle big time with languages and recognise it's a mental barrier more than anything else. I can communicate very basically in Thai but given that I have lived here for 8 years, it should be much better. Keeping it written down remains my goal, but it is also my internal punishment.

Outside of my yearly goals, I also have my big goals, which I have written down and plan to do at some point, although the exact year isn't locked in yet. These are all adventure-related goals, such as seeing snow leopards and polar bears in the wild. I am not a big fan of fly-in/take the photo/fly-out again holidays. I like to do things a little differently. For example, I really wanted to see the Komodo Dragons in Indonesia in the wild. I could've flown from Singapore to Bali, then flown to Flores, and then arranged for a tour agent to see them (a 1-week trip). Instead, I ferried from Singapore with my bicycle to Batam to Jakarta and cycled, ferried, etc., to Flores, then found a local boat and visited Komodo. I then ferried and cycled as far as Dili/East Timor (> 2000 km cycling over a 6-week trip = adventure). It probably cost me the same $$$ too. It's nice to move out of one's comfort zone and adventure!

And some goals just disappear altogether and become just a new way of life. Drinking less alcohol has now turned into don't drink alcohol. Eating less red meat has now turned into not eating red meat. They are now natural behaviours for me now. No challenge to it!

I personally find writing down financial and other goals very rewarding. The key, I find, is ensuring you have a good sense of balance and are looking to embrace new challenges and change as a person (hopefully for the better) along the way. Financial Freedom planning is a key part of this journey, but what's really cool is that it doesn't make it boring. It actually makes the journey a lot more fun as it helps you to navigate and discover what's important to you along the way.

It also helps to ensure you don't leave everything to the end because you never know what's coming around that corner!! SMASH: A speeding bus. Oh no, someone just threw a snowball at me. Phew!!

Dietary Advice (couldn't resist – sorry!): Diet = yuk. I would like to make this a swear word. Dxxx! Statistically, when people go on diets, after a while, the weight loss returns: a diet = a short-term goal? A while back, there was a TV reality show called "The Biggest Loser" about who would lose the most body weight % over a few weeks, and the winner would get some prize money I guess. Apparently, most of them regained the weight loss a few years later. Need to lose weight? Don't Dxxx: instead, make the required changes part of your lifestyle. After a while, they just become a natural part of your daily/weekly routine.

39. It's your turn to add some guiding principles.

I can't think of any more to add. Over to you! There are likely a few good (or bad) habits you have already that may not fall directly under the above. Add them to the list and be mindful of them.

To summarise:

Make your Financial Freedom plan.

Work out what works best for you.

Stick to having a plan (although the plan may change many times).

Work hard and smart to keep moving forward career-wise.

Save that money and get that money working for you.

Embrace balance.

Have fun.

(Damn, I could have written this on a Post-it note!)

NOW FOR THE MECHANICS OF THE PLAN:

1. Expense tracker.

The first step is quite simple. Create your expense tracker. You should review it monthly until you are comfortable with finding your groove, and then perhaps just review quarterly or annually. You need to capture:

How much do you earn?
How much do you spend?
How much do you save?
If you are not saving, then why not? And what do you need to change?
If you are saving, then are you saving enough? If not, then why not? What do you need to change?
Your planned savings then get input into your Financial Freedom roadmap.

Your template should look something like the following: apologies if the data used, appears somewhat inaccurate in a few places. I tried to base it on a 25-year-old, maybe in the U.S., I Googled some of the average costs – some of them I didn't Google: lazy thumb syndrome – (yes, I type with my thumbs).

Note: Add more lines to match your situation; for example, if you have more than one income/other kinds of debt/you may own your property (so you need to add house insurance, council rates, property maintenance, etc.)

Expense Tracker updated	1/1/2025	
INCOME	per month	per year
base salary	4000	48000
bonus	583	7000
gross income	4583	55000
tax	917	11000
NET income	**3667**	**44000**
EXPENSES	per month	per year
rent	1700	20400
power & water	120	1440
food	500	6000
car insurance & mtce	165	1980
petrol	100	1200
holiday	200	2400
fitness	50	600
phone and wifi	85	1020
alcohol	100	1200
cigarettes	100	1200
personal insurance	200	2400
coffee fix	90	1080
other **STUFF**	320	3840
Total cost of living	3730	44760
Potential saving	**-63**	**-760**
DEBT	per month	per year
student loan	300	3600
car	340	4080
Debt repayments	**640**	**7680**
	per month	per year
Total expense	4370	52440
NET income	3667	44000
NET SAVING	**-703**	**-8440**
	-19.2%	-19.2%
TARGET	750	**9000**
	20%	of net income

In this above example, the person (who we will call Smokie - my childhood cat's name)) isn't doing very well. He is so far away from his target of saving 20% of his income. He has $8440/year more expenses than he is saving, so he has some tough choices to make. Typically, we might think, well, I need to earn more income, so I get a second job. That's possibly part of the solution, but the easiest and quickest part of the solution is to ask yourself some serious questions, such as:

Is my current job/salary aligned with my skill sets and experience and my value proposition? If YES, then I need to sort out my expenses. If NO, then I need to work on how to improve that, BUT it's not going to happen overnight. Meanwhile, I still have some unfavourable expenses.

Hmmm, where to cut back???

Rent: do I downsize/move back in with the folks/take in a flatmate?

Power and water: turn the lights off when not needed?

Holiday: Can I justify an overseas holiday this year until I get on top of my expenses?

Fitness: how often do I really go to the gym? Could I replace gym workouts with outdoor exercise like running?

Cigarettes: that is literally money going up in smoke. Give it up? (more on this later).

Alcohol: I need some of this in my life as that's my social fun – but maybe I cut back, maybe I don't go out on Wednesdays anymore? Maybe I get a little bit tipsy at home before I go out? Maybe I won't buy that expensive kebab (and chips and more chips) on the way home as I don't really need food at 1 am in the morning.

Personal insurance: Yes, I need this, but are there other options available? Can I get it through work?

Other STUFF: Do I need to buy the latest this and that brand?? What if I buy a second-hand for a while?

Coffee fix = the coffee equation: more on this later.

Car = YIKES... in the above example, the car costs (insurance/petrol/debt) approximately $605/month ($7260/year). That's almost all my negative savings. I still have 4 years to pay it off, and that's over $16k in repayment fees at 7% interest. (Reference back to good debt/bad debt). Do I even need a car? If yes, then what sort of car do I need? I lost 20% of the value when I drove my new car out of the car yard. If I sell my car now, what will it cost? Or am I best to pay off as much of the 7% loan now with some savings I have stashed away? Can I pay off the debt and buy me a decent enough second-hand car?

If the above model reflects your current position, then you are going to struggle to get ahead, and you will not be able to get your Financial Freedom plan moving forward until you make the required adjustments.

OK, let's assume some tough decisions have been made by Smokie (the cat?), and it now looks like the following:

Expense Tracker updated	1/6/2025	
INCOME	per month	per year
base salary	4000	48000
bonus	583	7000
gross income	4583	55000
tax	917	11000
NET income	**3667**	**44000**
EXPENSES	per month	per year
rent	1400	16800
power & water	100	1200
food	500	6000
car insurance & mtce	165	1980
petrol	100	1200
holiday	70	840
fitness	50	600
phone and wifi	85	1020
alcohol	50	600
cigarettes	0	0
personal insurance	170	2040
coffee fix	0	0
other **STUFF**	270	3240
Total cost of living	2960	35520
Potential saving	**707**	**8480**
DEBT	per month	per year
student loan	300	3600
car	100	1200
Debt repayments	**400**	**4800**
	per month	per year
Total expense	3360	40320
NET income	3667	44000
NET SAVING	**307**	**3680**
	8.4%	8.4%
TARGET	750	**9000**
	20%	of net income

Smokie (the cat) has embraced some lifestyle changes as follows: Smokie, what changes did you make?

I moved into a slightly smaller apartment - I now save $300 per month.

I use less power as I turn the lights off when not in the room, and I don't use the heating as much - that saves $20 per month.

My holiday budget was reduced by $130 per month. I can't justify too many big holidays until I get my budget sorted.

Fitness – I thought about cancelling my gym subscription, but it's something that gives me a good mental break from work, so I will keep it for now.

Alcohol – I cut back on the Wednesday night sessions and get a wee bit tipsy at home before I go out, and I don't midnight kebab it anymore - that saves $50 per month.

Cigarettes = gone. Should have done this years ago - that saves $100 per month.

Personal insurance is now done through work - that saves $30 per month.

Other STUFF – cut back on buying stuff - that saves $50 per month.

Coffee fix – I take my coffee at work and at home on the weekends - that saves $90 per month.

Smokie saves on these above items a total of $770 per month.

Smokie ended up selling his new car and bought a second-hand car, but he's still got a little debt that will be paid off in 2 years' time. He made some other lifestyle adjustments, too.

Cool! Smokie now saves potentially 8% of his salary.

He is still not at 20% of the salary-saving target, but if Smokie keeps a watchful eye on things, then he will get there soon. Smokie is expecting to get a salary adjustment soon (promotion due), and there is no need for Smokie to increase his expenses once that comes through and the car is debt-free in 2 years.

The **big question** now that these changes have been made is: SMOKIE, is your life better or worse because of the above changes????

"Hmmm, well, I am still enjoying life and having fun with friends, so NOPE, giving up on some things hasn't made anything worse. In fact, I probably think it's cooler as I don't smoke, I drink less, I am more alert as a result of that at work (which I now take more seriously), and I still catch up with cool friends (and spend less time with the more drink culture friends which is OK with me). Swapped my ski trip to Whistler in Canada with a cycling/camping trip through Colorado with my partner, which I am super excited about (and it saves me $$$). Oh, and I am no longer a coffee snob. None of these changes feel like any extra hassle!! I still have my student debt to navigate but am looking at options on how to reduce that – it will take a bit more time."

What's cool now is I got this tracked, and my Excel brain will kick in and kick me up the bum really hard if I am about to spend money on STUFF when STUFF isn't needed.

Alright, way to go, Smokie, who no longer smokes, but the name is still Smokie – and was a super cool cat! Meeeeoooooooowwwww

OK, hopefully, the above is quite clear.

And if not, then hopefully, this helps to make it clearer:

Sometimes, the best decision is the uncomfortable decision – and often, the uncomfortable decision didn't end up being uncomfortable at all - and you kick yourself in the bum about why that decision wasn't made a long time ago.

Choose your journey wisely!

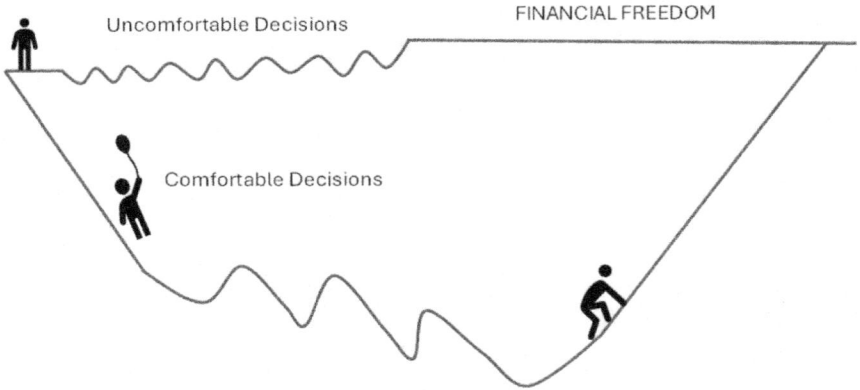

Uncomfortable Decisions

FINANCIAL FREEDOM

Comfortable Decisions

2. The Financial Freedom road map.

The following is an example template I made just now. It's similar to what I use, except I have different assets. I touched on the need to have such a plan earlier under Financial Freedom Planning but have placed it here as it nicely follows the expense tracker template.

The data you need to capture is essentially:

What equity (money) do I have today, and how much % return am I currently getting?

What is my targeted % return?

What is my savings per year forecast?

How old am I today?

When will I die?

When might I have my Financial Freedom?

And then just keep this updated. Recommend you keep it in one spreadsheet, and each year, simply add a new tab, e.g. if the next year is 2025, then copy/paste 2024 and keep it relevant.

There is also a column on inflation, which you need to be aware of.

It looks a little something like this (update this sheet every month or every 3 months):

(Note I trimmed the rows again for formatting purposes – each year = 1 row).

Updated	06/06/2024							
Net worth (1/1/2024)	**10000**							
Assets owned	Opening balance	% Portfolio	Target ROI	Target ROI	Target	% Portfolio	Current balance	Growth YTD
Emergency cash	2000	20%	0%	0	2000	19%	3250	1250
Term deposit cash	3000	30%	5%	150	3150	30%	3075	75
ETFs	5000	50%	9%	450	5450	51%	5250	250
Total	10000	100%	6%	600	10600	100%	11575	**1575**

Emergency salary has grown as it includes your savings year to date.

Savings increase/yr	$1,000						**3%**
	Open net worth	Target ROI	Target ROI	Income saving	Target Growth	Target net worth	Cost of living
25	**10,000**	**4%**	400	**3,680**	4,080	14,080	40,000
26	14,080	**5%**	704	4,680	5,384	19,464	41,200
27	19,464	**6%**	1,168	5,680	6,848	26,312	42,436
28	26,312	**7%**	1,842	6,680	8,522	34,834	43,709
29	34,834	**8%**	2,787	7,680	10,467	45,300	45,020
30	45,300	8%	3,624	8,680	12,304	57,604	46,371
35	128,316	8%	10,265	13,680	23,945	152,261	53,757
40	279,625	8%	22,370	18,680	41,050	320,676	62,319
45	531,282	8%	42,503	23,680	66,183	597,465	72,244
50	930,381	8%	74,431	28,680	103,111	1,033,492	83,751
55	1,546,122	8%	123,690	33,680	157,370	1,703,492	97,090
60	2,480,180	8%	198,414	38,680	237,094	2,717,275	112,554
65	3,881,951	8%	310,556	43,680	354,236	4,236,187	130,482
66	4,236,187	8%	338,895	-	338,895	4,575,082	134,396
70	5,763,286	8%	461,063		461,063	6,224,349	151,264
75	8,468,158	8%	677,453		677,453	9,145,611	175,356
80	12,442,503	8%	995,400		995,400	13,437,903	203,286
85	18,282,119	8%	1,462,569		1,462,569	19,744,688	235,664
90	26,862,430	8%	2,148,994		2,148,994	29,011,425	273,199

In the above scenario, you hit $3.8m around age 65 with a target growth in retirement of 338k per year (passive income + growth income). Based on the 3% inflation your expenses may be running around 134k/yr.

I also assumed a lower target ROI in the early years as it might take some time to ramp up your investments. And it is capped at 8% as you will always need to keep some cash holdings.

I have used conservative data above, as I would like to think you can increase your salary savings by more than $1k per year, and the more you save/invest, the less % of your overall net worth is required as emergency cash.

Each person's roadmap will be different, but the key here is that you have a plan. Keep track of it as things change, as it takes time to understand the sort of person you are when it comes to money and saving and investing. This approach will significantly help you to achieve your Financial Freedom based on the targets you set, and it ensures you are ready for those yukky surprises that you may have taken for granted, e.g.

What - no Government pension?

What - my insurance didn't cover me falling off Mt Everest?

What - inflation. I thought it was a myth?

What – my kid is now 27 years old, and I still need to buy him an iPhone, iPad and a MacBook?

You can run many scenarios - What if I just hold off providing a house for my kids until I am 80 years old as opposed to 65 years old – then I will have a lot more breathing space, and my kids can get an even bigger house.

My equivalent spreadsheet has a first tab of 1996, and with a little bit of luck, my last tab will be at least the year 2057 (and beyond if I can get some cyber chips inserted).

3. What to invest in.

Well, this is a multiple-book topic within itself, so I will try to keep it relatively brief, along with what I focus on these days. There are so many options out there, and it can get confusing, so I will try to present a simple, balanced starting point. However, the key here is to do your research and do due diligence.

This next blurb is what I borrowed from Google.

Asset Overview.

Traditional assets

* *Stocks and bonds are among the most commonly known investments. Along with cash, these are known as traditional investments.*

* *Stocks give shareholders a share of ownership in a company. Investors purchase stocks hoping they will go up in price, earn dividend payments (if the company distributes some of its earnings to stockholders), vote for shares and influence company decisions. Stocks can be categorized in many ways, including growth stocks (where investors hope the company and stock price grow rapidly), income stocks (where investors seek consistent income), and value stocks (where investors seek stable returns). They can also be classified by size: Large caps (the largest-size companies), mid-caps (relatively medium-sized companies), and small caps (the smallest companies). Stocks are generally considered to have more risk and return potential compared with bonds.*

* *Bonds are debt investments—similar to an IOU. Borrowers sell bonds to raise money for a certain amount of time. When you buy a bond, you are entitled to receive a specified rate of interest during the life of the bond and to receive back your original*

investment (also known as the principal or face value) when the bond comes due after a set period of time. Types of bonds include Government, municipal, and corporate. They can be categorized in different ways, including investment grade (i.e., those that have a higher credit rating implying they are relatively less risky) and high yield (i.e., those that have a lower credit rating implying they are relatively riskier).

- *Stocks and bonds are the most common components in mutual funds and exchange-traded funds (ETF's), which are baskets of investments combined into a single investment option. Mutual funds and ETFs pool money from many investors and invest all that money collectively. Investors can buy shares in a mutual fund or ETF, with each share representing part ownership in the fund. Among the differences between these 2 investment choices: ETF share prices fluctuate during the day on a stock exchange, while mutual funds are valued at the end of the trading day. Because they are baskets of investments, mutual funds and exchange-traded funds may help you more easily build a diversified portfolio.*

- *Options are another type of investment that commonly utilizes traditional investments. Options are contracts that give buyers the right and sellers an obligation to buy and sell an underlying asset (such as a stock) at a specified price, up and until a specified date. Options contracts are listed on the option chain— a list of all the options available for an underlying investment.*

Alternative assets

- *Alternative assets are investments that are relatively more complex and less liquid (i.e., not as easy to buy or sell) compared with traditional investments. It's important to understand that there are more risks with these relatively complex investment types and that they are not suitable for all investors. Types of alternative assets include hedge funds, real assets, private equity, and structured products.*

- *Hedge funds are the largest category among alternative assets. A hedge fund is a privately organized investment vehicle that is less regulated by the Government than traditional funds, enabling it to invest using a wide variety of strategies in nearly any investable asset. This group also includes managed futures, which is a type of hedge fund that invests in futures contracts— commonly stock, bond, commodity, and currency futures.*

- *Real assets are investments in assets through direct ownership and not via financial assets (e.g., stocks). Natural resources, commodities, real estate, infrastructure, and intellectual property are the most prevalent real assets. Examples of natural resources are water and timber. Commodities—which differ from natural resources in that they are extracted, mined, or produced—are homogenous and available in large quantities. Examples are oil, gas, coal, gold, silver, copper, steel, iron, and livestock. Real estate is land and improvements that are affixed—like houses or office buildings. (Note: Real estate investment trusts, commonly known as REITs, can be viewed as a traditional investment).*

- *Private equity invests in stock or bond positions that are not publicly traded. Private equity investments typically involve financing higher-risk start-up companies.*

- *Structured products are investments that are created to generate a specific return, risk, taxation, or other attribute. They include credit derivatives, annuities, and other products.*

- *Of course, the list of alternative assets is not restricted to these categories—it can essentially include anything that is not a traditional investment. Rare art, collectables, and other tradeable assets are additional examples of alternative assets.*

More recently, cryptocurrencies like Bitcoin, Ethereum, and Tether—have gained widespread attention.

OK, thanks, Google – now, back to my take on the above:

Remember how I recommend investing in things you are interested in and understand. Investing should be seen differently from trading. Trading typically implies a buy and a sell over a shorter period. For example, you can buy a Microsoft share at $400 in the morning and hope to sell it for $430 in the afternoon. There are different forms of trading (day trading/swing trading/option calls/selling puts), and they can include things like trading in stocks, forex (foreign currency), and cryptos. There are so many different strategies, but what's clear is that none of them work all the time. If they did work all the time, then we would have trillionaires (which we don't!). They come with high risk/high reward, but often, the person making the money is the one selling the trading strategy. Let's face it: if you had an amazingly successful winning trading strategy, would you bother to set up training classes on this and sell Patreon membership subscriptions for maybe $100/month when your strategy is so amazingly successful that after 12 months with a 95% win rate, you should have grown your initial $1000 to be making $10million/month. I have dabbled in a few of these trading strategies over time. None have been long-term successful, but I have only allocated a super small $ amount to them and wasn't expecting them to change my life. I won't be focusing on trading as we are focused on Financial Freedom, which requires investing and typically implies a longer-term allocation of money.

Property vs. stocks/ETFs and the liquidity mind game.

Property is typically considered a longer-term investment. We don't buy property in the morning and sell it in the afternoon. When we buy property, we automatically think of a 5-year, 10-year or 20-year+ time frame. The property doesn't have the liquidity of stocks/ETFs. If I want to sell my property, I typically need to engage a real estate agent. We agree on the target sell price, the commission, and what to do if it currently has tenants. Will we sell it directly based on appointment viewing, or will we have an open home or auction it? When it is sold, we need to have a sales agreement and a property lawyer involved, and the money is typically received back in my account a while after the sales agreement is signed and the property is sold. The frustrating thing about property is it doesn't have immediate liquidity.

BUT the great thing about property is that it doesn't have immediate liquidity. You own a property but need to sell it. You need the cash now! It ain't going to happen. We don't know the exact market value of the property and what it would sell for. We only ever know a range. You bought a property 5 years ago for $400k. Today, your property may sell for between $500k - $550k. But we can't be sure, and if we put it on the market today by the time it gets ready to sell and find a buyer, maybe the property market has gone down, and maybe we can only get $480k for it (or maybe it has gone up, and we get lucky and sell it for $570k. Because it doesn't have immediate liquidity, it doesn't play with your emotional idiot brain as much. We don't know the exact value of the property, and if we did, we couldn't sell it immediately, so our brain is naturally wired to be more accepting and less stressed over movements up and down in the value of our property – and so by default, we tend to hold property investments much longer and over time residential property typically goes up quite well in value (just not always in a straight line).

But instead of buying that property, consider that you bought Microsoft stock at $400/share. You bought 1000 shares x $400 = $400k. Same $value as invested in the above property. And your investment strategy was to hold Microsoft for 10 to 20 years. But Microsoft stock is totally liquid. You can immediately sell it during business hours on a weekday, and you know exactly what you can sell it for. So, you buy Microsoft for $400/share, and after 3 months, it has dropped to $370/share. That's -$30k that you have lost! Oh, no, this is really stressing you out. Next week, it has dropped to $360/share. That's now -$40k that you have lost. Shhhhiiiiitttt. Next week, it is down to $350/share. That's now -$50k that you have lost. Super stressful now. Next week, it has gone back to $360/share. OK, you have pegged back $10k. You don't want to risk losing any more, so you sell at $360/share, and phew, you only lost $40k (not $50k), and now the stress is over, and you are pissed off you lost $40k, but hey it could've been a lot worse. So, you can see the downside of having immediate liquidity. You know exactly what the value of that investment is at any given time, and because you can exit it at any given time, the emotional rollercoaster with our idiot brain is a lot more challenging.

What about this approach?

When you bought your property at $400k, you did a lot of due diligence on why that property, in that neighbourhood, at that price with expected rental income and loan repayments, etc. You have good conviction that it's a good investment and planned to hold it for 10+years

When you bought Microsoft at $400/share, you did a lot of due diligence on why that company, based on its fundamentals and

114

perceived stock value. You have good conviction that it's a good investment and planned to hold it for 10+ years.

So, what changed: Microsoft may have gone down to $350/share, but so did all the other large tech companies go down by the same %. This was simply a market re-correction of 12.5%. What happened to your conviction that, over 10+ years, this would be a good investment?

Your property value may have dropped to 360k also, but you may not be aware of that because you can't log into Yahoo Finance and search for your property's exact value every day.

Emotion plays a bigger role in investing, and one of the key things to learn and assess is your own personal investment behaviour.

Sometimes, people buy stocks when the price is way too high = FOMO.

Sometimes, people sell stocks when they have gone down in price = PANIC.

FOMO and PANIC aren't good investing tools, especially when they get manipulated by media NOISE. On any given day, my news feeds will show totally opposite headlines: "Market crash is coming," "Recession is just around the corner," or "Bank XYZ predicts the S&P 500 will hit new highs next quarter." So, who to listen to to? For me, the answer is "None of them."

In the above scenario, if I owned 400k of Microsoft and it went down to $350/share, and if there was nothing specific to Microsoft but was a tech stock re-correction, then if I had cash available, I would simply have bought some more Microsoft stock. I get a decent discounted share price, and my conviction to hold for 10+ years remains unchanged.

Oh, fast forward time travel to 2 years later, Microsoft is trading at $460/share. Hmmm, that's 60k > more than the initial investment = Shit; you shouldn't have sold at $360.

NOW, I have used Microsoft above as an example that hopefully is easily relatable, BUT if I had 400k and it was the majority of my net worth, although I may put it into 1 property, I would NEVER put it into 1 stock. I would look to spread that $400k across maybe 20 stocks. Protects me by having diversification, and not all of those stocks would be tech stocks (diversification within diversification), or I would invest the majority of the 400k into ETFs.

But before I move on to stocks and ETFs, I will focus a bit more on property.

Property:

The downside of property is that to buy property, you need to have a decent amount of money (deposit) to start with. For a 400k property, you probably need about $100k+. That can take a while to save up. However, for stocks, you can typically open a trading account for free and start investing for as little as $100. The benefit, of course, is that you can get your money working for you a lot quicker than when you save up for that initial property. But you should have property on your roadmap either as your home (save on rent and a good long-term investment) or for rental income (rents typically increase and a good long-term investment).

I am comfortable loaning money from a bank to buy a property. Now I have someone else's money (thank you bank) working for me!

I would NEVER loan money from anyone to invest in stocks/ETFs. Some brokers will let you leverage (borrow) money to buy stocks/ETFs, and this is something I would never endorse – **big** due diligence is required on this one.

Property Considerations: There are quite a few things to consider when buying a property, and I won't cover all of them, but some of the things to be mindful of are:

Residential versus commercial property. Commercial property is typically rented out as shops and businesses, and typically, a lot of the property's operating expenses are covered by the commercial renter. The rents are typically higher, so you tend to get a better % yield return on a commercial property versus a residential property. However, sometimes the commercial property is more difficult to rent out, or sometimes the 'business district' that the commercial property resides in could have a bit of a downturn, so it does come with a little more risk. Due Diligence is required.

Getting quality tenants. I bought a lower-cost property once, and even though the rents were relatively low, it was still a cash flow positive investment, BUT because the rents were low, my tenants were absolute shits and drew on the walls, punched a wall in and took some metal piping from the internal heating. I sold that property and took a slight loss on it. Not worth the headache of shit tenants. It would be better to buy in a slightly better neighbourhood at a higher price, higher rent (still positive cash flow), and better quality tenants. Ideal tenants are the mum + dad + 2 kids scenario, I guess.

Tax laws: many countries have capital gains tax on property. You buy for $400k. You sell for $520k. After expenses, your net gain is $100k. You may have to pay tax on that $100k. You still made money, but make sure you factor these potential taxes into your return on investment.

Condominium/apartments versus a house: Condos will have body corporate/management fees, which you pay monthly (or quarterly) to cover the costs of communal facilities (e.g., car parking/building outside maintenance/swimming pool/gardening, etc.). This is typically factored into the rent you charge, so you should still have a positive cash flow, BUT you want to ensure the management team maintaining the property is professional and doing a good job and that the management fees don't keep increasing too much (or that they run out of cash?). In Thailand, I bought my apartment when it was about 20 years old. It has been very well maintained, management fees have remained in line with the market, and no fees have gone missing. I would be hesitant to buy an apartment off the plan in Thailand as although the end product may be great, there is a higher risk it will look run-down after 12-24 months (if the management team is crap). It's a risk to be considered when doing your due diligence. I bought my apartment, which backs onto a golf course. I don't play golf, but I know my view will remain. Nothing worse than buying into that new development with a beach view, and then, just as your development is completed, they start building another condo right in front of yours. So, you can buy a new condo with a beautiful beach view that is guaranteed for 6 months only. Other countries have better governance than Thailand, so that is a factor when investing in property.

Interest rates: When you buy a property, what's really good is that you don't need 100% of the money as you can get a loan (mortgage) from the bank. That is really cool, as you are leveraging the banks money to work for you. As your property goes up in value, you don't need to give any of that increased value to the bank, so it's really beneficial. But when you take a loan from the bank, you have to pay interest on the money you are borrowing. There are fixed and variable options on the % interest you need to pay. The main challenge you have is that interest rates can move up and down, and if you have a 300k mortgage on a 400k property, then at 3% interest, that's $9k/year, you have to pay just in interest. No sweat, as the rent you are receiving is still cash flow positive, including the $9k interest. But what if the bank increases the interest to 5% then that's now $15k/year in interest. Still cash flow positive? Back in the 1970s and 80s, interest rates were >10% = 30k in interest per year = YIKES. Fortunately, Governments are much better these days at working with financial institutions to manage interest rates, but you need to ensure you have done your due diligence in this area. As a rule of thumb, I tend to put down a 33% deposit on a rental property instead of 20 to 25%. It means I may need to wait a little longer before buying the property, but it also means I have more breathing space in the event the interest rates increase on me and/or I can't find a tenant and/or rent goes down.

Renovations: It is likely you will need to do some renovations when buying a property, and if it is a new one, then certainly some furniture. It's important not to overspend here – even if this is your dream home because, ultimately, it should be considered an investment first. Here's a couple of tricks I have used:

If the property is a little bit older, then I would paint the walls and ceilings white and add a couple of large mirrors here and there. Mirrors make the rooms look bigger. White is neutral and won't put a tenant off (versus someone saying, "I really liked the place, but the big pink wall in the master bedroom just isn't my thing"). I would change the door handles, wall sockets, light switches, and kitchen cabinet handles. These are relatively cheap things to replace, but they immediately make the place look new. So, I have given the place a very fresh, updated look but have not spent a lot of money on it. If I am renting the place fully furnished, then I wouldn't spend a great deal on the furniture itself - Ikea style is good enough.

Where to buy the property: That is really going to depend on you. Most people buy property in their local area and/or in their country of residence. This makes the most common sense. Some buy property overseas and use it as a holiday home (and rent it out when not using it). I like to buy property with good governance and minimal surprises. For example, I knew someone who bought a new off-plan property in Bali. Turned out they owned the property legally, but the access (driveway) to their property was not part of the deal, so they had to negotiate that. In New Zealand, the typical length of time a property is on the market before it is sold is maybe 3 months. In Thailand, it may be 12+ months. When buying a property that has been on the market for 12+ months, you have good negotiating power, but you will be stuck with the same problem when you go to sell it. If you buy a property in a different country, you will have foreign exchange rate risks to consider. Pros and cons and lots of things to weigh up for consideration. The best thing is to create a table in Excel and write out the advantages/disadvantages so you can take a more balanced view as opposed to "Wow, I am going to live the dream life in my dream home in Bali = shit: I can't get to my property as the driveway is blocked and what happened to the beach view."

Here is an Excel sheet on property mathematics (to ensure it is cash flow positive).

Purchase price	400,000	
Legal fees	2,500	1
Renovations	10,000	2
Furniture	8,000	3
Total	**420,500**	
Deposit 1	20,500	Items 1,2,3 above
Deposit 2	120,000	30%
Total cash outlay	140,500	
Bank loan	280,000	Purchase price minus deposit 2
Years	25	loan term
Interest rate	3.0%	per annum

	Per month	Per year
Loan repayment	933	11,200
Interest	700	8,400
Bank repayment	1,633	19,600

Income	Per month	Per year
Rent Gross	2080	24960

Expenses	Per month	Per year	
Agent commission	83	998	4%
Council fees	104	1250	
Insurance	83	1000	
Maintenance etc	129	1550	
Total expense	400	4798	

Expenses + Loan	2,033	24,398	
Income	2,080	24,960	
Cashflow	47	562	

Net Cashflow	47	562	
Tax	5	56	10%
After Tax	42	505	

	Per year
Net income	505
Loan repayment	11,200
Total income	11,705
Total cash outlay	140,500
Net return on cash	8.33%

This excludes any value increase in the property price.

*Net income is the positive cash flow per year: This example is just positive, but *loan repayment is the tenant paying off your bank loan, which is good (just the 11,200 is not available for you as cash flow).

These numbers exclude any value increase in the property.

Note to break even on the purchase price of the property, you will need to sell it at $437718 as shown below (and check if your country has capital gains tax on any profit you make on the sale of your property – if there is a tax then that may not be a bad thing as it does imply you made a profit).

Total property cost	420,500	
Agent commission	14,718	4%
Legal fees	2,500	
Break even sell price	**437,718**	

Note: If the interest rate stays constant, then over time, the interest paid reduces as you reduce your loan amount.

The above scenario has a positive cash flow. I would add an extra 3% deposit, though. By making this template before I go to look at properties, I save a lot of time because I can limit the properties to be viewed within my $$ boundary range.

In Summary, If you do solid due diligence, then property is a very good and proven investment. However, due diligence is very important because there is a saying that goes, "There is never a bad time to buy a property - only a bad time to sell one." You don't want to be forced to sell a property in a bad market because you didn't have enough cash flow breathing space (e.g., increased interest rates/no tenant/reduced rents).

However, having a property rental does require more work as you either manage it directly, or you have an agent. And you have to pay council tax, insurance, tax returns, etc. It's quite a bit more hands-on than some of the other investments.

As you get older, you may find this is a great thing to spend your time on, OR you may find it a pain in the bum. I have a smaller property portfolio these days as I have gotten too lazy to be distracted by the overseeing of them.

Stocks and ETFs.

Which one? U.S. or Europe or Australia or China or emerging markets?? Out of the 10,000 companies, which stock do I buy, and do I focus on growth or dividend stocks or the energy sector versus the tech sector? Do I focus on big companies or small companies? Or do I buy stocks or mutual funds or ETFs and call options and puts?

There is no correct answer, as it depends on things like your risk appetite, your base currency, tax stuff, etc. This is something you will have to research yourself, but here are some key points specific to the stock market, and then I will briefly indicate what has (and should continue) to work for me.

Stocks are typically reflective of the publicly listed company, which is where you can buy a piece of that company. Buy Microsoft for $400, and Yep, you own a wee wee wee wee piece of Microsoft: Congratulations, you are a shareholder.

The U.S. stock market has historically been the best-performing market. This makes sense because you try to name some of the top companies from any country, and you get stuck quite quickly, but I bet you can rattle 25+ companies headquartered in the U.S. really quickly. So, by contrast, many U.S. companies are truly global. As a result, more money flows into the U.S. stock market than any other, and that includes foreign money, too. The New Zealand stock market, with only a population of 5 million, is never going to rock long term.

The S&P 500 (The Standard and Poor's 500) is a stock market index tracking the stock performance of 500 of the largest companies listed on stock exchanges in the United States. Some companies may drop out of the 500 (due to poor financial performance), and others may enter it (due to good financial performance). There is often a term used to "beat the market," and this is simply beating the overall performance of the S&P 500. The S&P started over 100 years ago, but it didn't start with 500 companies. Since 1957, it has returned an average of 10.3% per annum (this is about 6.4%, taking inflation into consideration). However, this is never in a straight line. 10% is the annualised average – some years, it has done negative (2008 financial crisis –36%) and most years, it has done positive (2013 +32%). But the key takeaway is historically, over time, it is positive, and no other country index (UK FTSE 100/Japan Nikkei/Singapore Strait Times/Australia ASX) has outperformed this over the long term. They may have a great year now and then, but not long-term in comparison. Off course, we don't know what lies ahead, but the S&P 500 has managed to muscle its way through some pretty shit times (The Great Depression/The Vietnam War/The 2000 Dot.com Crash/The 2008 Financial Crisis/Covid).

U.S. stocks are bought and sold in USD. That is still considered to be the default global base currency, so we don't feel too bad if we get stuck with the USD (versus the Venezuelan peso).

Out of these 500 stocks, which do I buy? There are all sorts of metrics you can look at in determining which stock to buy, and fortunately, all that information is available online and pretty much for free (some online sites are subscription-based, but I never pay for any subscriptions). A US public company reports its results every quarter, and there is a body called the SEC that audits and ensures the results are reported. This information is available online. You can do a lot of due diligence on existing public companies and use a whole lot of financial metrics to ascertain if a company such as Microsoft is a good company to buy. At a very high level, the things to focus on are increasing revenue, increasing profit, managing its debt, and managing available cash flow; it isn't increasing its number of shares, performing better or as well as its competitors, and often has a business moat (makes the company very hard to copy) and has a good leadership team. Some big companies I grew up with are no longer around (General Electric/Kodak/Enron/ Wang), so when choosing a stock to buy, it has to be a bit more than "Oh, that's a big company, and I have heard of them."

Some stocks pay a dividend, which is typically quarterly when you receive cash back from the stock you own. For example, if you bought Coca-Cola today (KO), it would cost you $68, and this year, you may receive $1.84 in cash, which is about a 2.7% dividend. Depending on where you are a tax resident, you likely have to pay a little withholding tax on that $1.84. Some companies pay higher dividends, and some companies pay no dividends or relatively small dividends. Amazon doesn't pay a dividend because it is still very focused on growth, as it wants to keep reinvesting its free cash flow back into growth. Apple pays a 0.5% dividend because it is still really focused on growth, but it recognises that it's cool for shareholders to also get some dividends. Coca-Cola pays about a 2.7% dividend because they recognise they probably won't grow at the same rate as they have done historically, so they would rather balance with less growth projection but, in return, hold onto shareholders by offering a higher dividend. Some companies offer much higher dividends of around 8 to 10%, which is great, but historically, they often have trouble with growth, so although you get an 8% dividend, the share price may fall 4% each year. Typically, younger investors seem to focus on growth, and older investors seem to focus on dividends.

So, with so many stocks to choose from, it can be hard to know which ones to select. If you approach a professional financial adviser, they will typically come up with a balanced stock portfolio where some of the stocks are tech (Microsoft), energy (Exxon), finance (JP Morgan), consumer (Home Depot), property Reits

(Realty Income) etc. and so you are not exposed to one company or one sector and should entail a mix of growth and dividends. Sounds good, right??

Quite some time ago (1924), a finance company came up with the idea that you could buy a basket of stocks and call them a mutual fund. These baskets are super varied and could include a basket like just mentioned above, or the basket could just focus on financial stocks or maybe just growth stocks or maybe just on the entire S&P500 index (i.e., you purchase 1 mutual fund, and you own a little bit of 500 companies).

In 1993, ETFs (Exchange Traded Funds) were created. They are essentially the same as a mutual fund, but the management fees are typically a lot less.

In the old days, if you wanted to buy a stock, you had to go to a stockbroker/financial adviser, and they would buy that stock for you, and you would pay them a fee for buying it (and probably managing it).

In the new days, it's pretty easy to set up an online broker account and do it yourself. There are some app-friendly stuff like RobinHood and WeeBull, as well as some well-established brokers like TD Waterhouse and Interactive Brokers. There are quite a few to choose from. I use **Interactive Brokers** – they have been around a long time and offer good security on my portfolio they hold, have been very responsive whenever I have had a question/easy to move money in and out (same business day), and their commission charges are very low. If I make a $100 buy on Coca-Cola, they will charge me $1 in commission. If I make a $10000 buy on Coca-Cola, they will charge me $1 in commission.

If investing for the long term then I recommend someone more secure like Interactive Brokers as opposed to the newer friendly phone apps.

A financial adviser versus a mutual fund versus an ETF versus which online broker account?

Some key points:

These are different stats from the internet, but somewhere between 75 and 80% of financial advisers do not beat the market (S&P 500), and yet there are fees paid to them. I started with a finance adviser, and they created a basket of balanced stocks; it performed OK, but I was paying a % management fee, and I was getting frustrated because they were really slow to react to things. They wouldn't proactively reinvest dividends. When they did buy some shares, it would cost about $8/trade (versus $1). I stuck with them for about 3 years as I knew nothing about stock valuations and portfolios when I started. And so it became a good way for me to get invested, learn about the markets, and learn about my temperament. Do I panic when stocks go down, or am I chilled? This was very important!

After 3 years, I had them transfer my portfolio to my new personal Interactive Brokers account I had set up and then started to self-manage it. I feel more comfortable managing it myself as I know my style.

Mutual funds are actively (or passively) managed baskets of stock you can buy rather than each stock being picked by the finance adviser. You are going to pay an annual fee typically > 0.5% for a passive fund and >1% for an active fund, plus there may be some other fees involved when you top up and buy and sell.

ETFs are pretty much the same as mutual funds, **BUT** they are typically much more efficiently managed. Some ETFs do come with a management fee of 1%, BUT there are some awesome ETFs with a management fee of <0.1%. One ETF we will cover later is SPLG, and its management fee is 0.02%. When I buy it on Interactive Brokers, I only pay a $1 total commission. ($1 if I buy $100 worth or $1 if I buy $10000 worth). There was a bit of a commission war a few years ago as more online broker-related apps became available, which reduced the commissions = cool!

Why didn't my 'financial adviser' or any others recommend ETFs? Well, if they recommended ETFs, you would pretty quickly work out that maybe you don't need their services?

Mutual funds still play a role for the gen that isn't quite ready to 'just do it' yourself.

ETFs and your own broker account are a no-brainer these days for someone just starting out.

Remember, every 1% saved when compounded is awesome.

If I invest $100k and pay a 1% management fee to a financial adviser or a mutual fund. That's $1000 in fees. If I held this for 20 years, that would be compounded to $22130 in fees.

If I invest $100k in SPLG (S&P 500 tracker) ETF, I will pay a 0.02% management fee. That's $20 in fees. And if I held this for 20 years, that's compounded to $400 in fees.

That's a big difference in fees, and remember, 70-80% of the financial advisers don't beat the S&P500 anyway...

I have slowly moved my Stock portfolio into a mix of ETFs and Stocks. I am moving to about 50% ETFs and 50% stocks. I keep some individual stocks because I have done my own research and am confident the company will continue to grow, but I have balanced this out with ETFs, which I feel more comfortable with.

Getting Started: Hmmmm, starting out in the stock market could seem a little overwhelming. **But it's actually quite simple.**

1: Set up an online broker account. Interactive Brokers is a good choice as you can trade a wide range of country stocks on it (but there are many to choose from, and it may depend on where you live).

2: If you are comfortable with USD stocks, then maybe buy SPLG (or VOO), as these are reliable, low-cost S&P500 index trackers. At 10% historic returns per annum, you can double your money every 7ish years. If you want to mix it up a little, then look at SCHD, which is focused more on dividends; SCHG, which is focused more on growth; and XLK (or VGT), which is more tech-focused. There are a few tech overlaps in these ETFs, but that's hard to avoid because tech stocks make up such a large piece of the U.S. market (Microsoft/Google/Amazon/Apple/Nvidia/META, etc.).

Starting with $2000, you could simply go:

SPLG $800
SCHD $500
SCHG $500
XLK $200

Or whatever mix fits your style.

This mix, on average over the last 10 years, gives an annual return of about 14% return (double your money every 5.2 years). And if you keep adding to that (dollar-cost averaging) every quarter, then this should grow very nicely for you. (Remember, the above is based on historic averages = with no guarantee of future performance. Do your own due diligence. I am not a financial adviser, so the above is for entertainment purposes only (phew!!)) I don't work on the 14%, and I think that 10% is more practical over time.

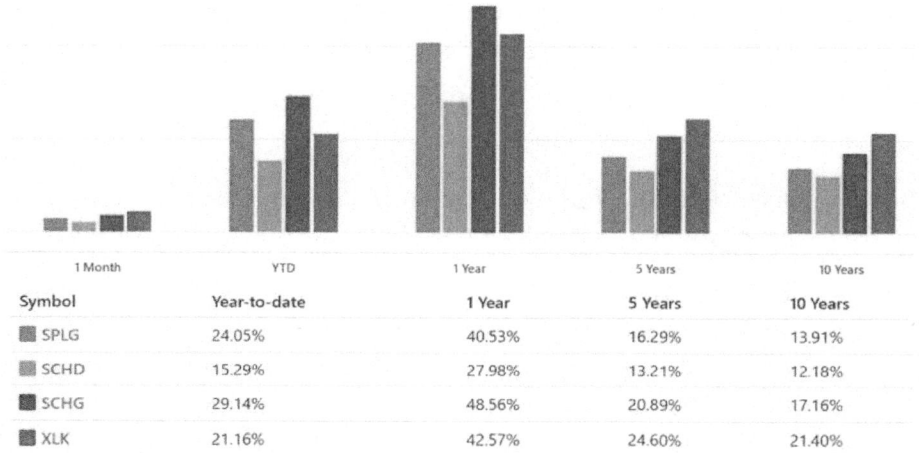

Symbol	Year-to-date	1 Year	5 Years	10 Years
SPLG	24.05%	40.53%	16.29%	13.91%
SCHD	15.29%	27.98%	13.21%	12.18%
SCHG	29.14%	48.56%	20.89%	17.16%
XLK	21.16%	42.57%	24.60%	21.40%

The above chart shows the SPLG/SCHD/SCHG/XLK historic returns as at October 2024. The %'s are annualised = average per year returns.

Or perhaps just buy SPLG (or VOO) and then analyse your behaviour over the first 3 to 6 months.

If you are not comfortable with US exposure, then research your own country for some local ETFs. But watch out for fees and performance; for example, here in Thailand, the stocks don't perform as well, and the fees are higher than my U.S. stuff. In Australia, there are a few very good ETFS (VLC A200 and VHY) that have reasonably low fees, track elements the ASX Index, and pay around 4% dividends, and you buy them in AUD. UK and Europe have their own ETFs, in GBP or Euro. You can also buy some US ETFS in GBP and Euro. There are also some global index tracking ETFs such as VWRL (which has U.S, Europe and Asia exposure), which you can buy in GBP or Euro. There is also a global tracker BGBL, which you can buy in AUD. These are easy enough to Google, depending on your own scenario.

When I research ETFs, I use a mix of 'trading view' and 'etf.com' and 'bar chart' and 'stock analysis.' All have subscription options, but I just use their free offerings. YouTube also has decent information/comparisons on them.

If you want to learn more about how to analyse a company or an ETF as a potential investment, then I would recommend <u>Learn to Invest - Investors Grow - YouTube.</u> Lots of good short educational videos without the 'hype to the moon type stuff." Out of courtesy, I reached out to Jimmy, who runs it, and asked if I could link his site to this book (without him reading my book), and he was supportive of that. I learnt a lot from his site when I first started out analysing stocks.

Remember, stocks/ETFs don't grow in a straight line. Starting with just these ETFS does give you time to learn about your investment style. If your ETF goes down 10% and you can't sleep and are so stressed, then maybe it's not the right form of investment for you. If it goes up 10% and you sell because you are nervous it will come back down, then maybe it's not the right form of investment for you. This year (Aug 2024), the stock market pulled back on average (in the tech sector) by about 8%. I watched my portfolio reduce, which is yuk, BUT I was also happy because it meant I could buy more of my favourite ETFs at an 8% discount. The stock market bounced back again at the end of Aug 2024. (so, I made 8% on paper, but it's not a real gain because I don't plan to sell those August ETF top-ups any time soon).

Hopefully, what happens for you is that you have invested in ETFs and you find them very interesting. You want to try other ETFs or invest in some stocks directly. Then that's great as you are investing in things you are interested in. Just remember to do your due diligence on the stocks/ETFs, and greed can be the killer.

Lump Sum Investing versus Dollar Cost Averaging: When starting to invest in Stocks/ETFs it can be difficult for idiot brain when you have a large lump sum of money and you want to invest it now **BUT** the market is at an all-time high. We get concerned/anxious that by buying at the TOP then the markets will slide down quite a bit and it will take a long time to get back to our original entry point. So, we are tempted to just hold off a bit for the markets to drop and then enter......... but then what if the markets don't drop and we watch the markets go up and up and up and shit we have missed the boat!

There is a good saying which is "time in the market BEATs timing the market" so if you are investing for the long term (5+ 10+ 20+ years) it's OK to invest that lump sum (or maybe you want to invest 50% today/25% next month/25% next month). There is no secret recipe here and you just have to go with what you feel comfortable with and recognise the potential ups and downs of your decision. If it is an initial lump sum but then you plan to 'top up' the investment with new savings every quarter (dollar cost averaging) then investing 100% of the lump sum today will not be as stressful.

My partner has a great recipe: She never started with a lump sum but started with a quarterly sum. Every quarter she invests some $$$s into the ETFs above and she doesn't really care about the price – as she is only thinking long term. She may top up a little bit more on one of the above ETFs if it is a little further down from its 52 week high (highest price in the last 12 months).

Back testing surveys have shown that if you have $120k to invest then investing it as a lump sum of $120k statistically is more likely to provide better long term results versus investing it as $10k/month spread out over 12 months. Sometimes it just comes down to good luck versus bad luck on timing BUT long term it should all morph into good luck.

October 2024: Last Tuesday, I sat with a friend I trail run with. He is 40. He knew about the stock markets but had no idea how to wade through all the noise and get started. On Thursday, he applied for his Interactive Brokers account, and it was completed by Saturday with some money now sitting in it. By Monday he had bought his first ETF(s). He was all set up within a week. He plans to invest a fixed amount regularly every 2 months. He will open some sub-accounts for his two young kids – that to me, is a very sound strategy. It did cost him a 'chai yen' iced tea drink for my management fee though (0.75c)

Other investment things.

I won't spend much time on them as they aren't really my thing, but I will give you some personal experience.

Government and Corporate bonds. I owned some of these when my financial adviser set up my balanced portfolio. They were paying about 6% dividend equivalent. I exited them when I set up Interactive Brokers directly. They pay a good dividend/coupon, but there isn't price growth in bonds.

You buy for $100. You hold for 5 years. You sell for $100. Your 6% dividend/coupon is fixed at 6% per annum.

I swapped them out for SCHD (3.5% dividend) and VLC.AX (5% dividend) as these ETFs also have some price growth. And I have no idea what the bond % dividend will be in 5 years' time (maybe interest rates are up or maybe they are down, so I will have a 'reinvestment decision' to make then). SCHD and VLC.AX dividends have been growing. So, I take a little less dividend passive income now, but in 5 years, the passive income equivalent should be more than the bond equivalent, and I have a high chance of growth (and yes, a risk of not growing or going negative), but this is part (and not ALL) of my portfolio so I still feel balanced). As I get much older, maybe bonds will become my thing (but I suspect not)!

Crypto – I invested a little bit into crypto about 4 years ago, and it just really isn't my thing. In November 2024 I sold out of my crypto completely. Overall, I made a small profit but as I didn't plan to invest any more money into it then for me it was an unnecessary distraction. Why not my thing? I can't analyse it. I can run numbers on a property and physically see the asset. Stocks I can review SEC reports and wade through all sorts of data on how the company is doing. Crypto = nope! So many theories on why this one is going to be awesome, world-changing blah, blah, blah hype, but no facts to support it. It mostly trades on noise. If I don't understand it, then I am not interested in it. If crypto is your thing, then that's great, but please ensure your overall portfolio is balanced beyond crypto.

Foreign Currency (Forex): I tried day trading this but couldn't find a consistent strategy, and that meant the win-to-loss ratio was never stable enough for me to make big trades. At best, I was doing maybe a $100 trade, but I would never have the confidence to increase those trade sizes, which meant I would be spending a lot of time on not much return potential.

Gold/Silver: This works for some people. I have never owned any. It's not a thing I am interested in.

Fine art and old collectable sports cars: Luckily I don't have a garage.

To summarise, what has worked for me has been property and stocks/ETFs (predominantly U.S. stuff). I keep a fairly balanced portfolio as I hold equity in USD/AUD/NZD/Euro/SGD and THB. (mine is a little more complicated because I have lived and earnt in different countries)

I hold some cash, and I derive passive income (which is comfortably more than my living expenses) from property rental and dividends. I am comfortable that my net worth will continue to grow more than my living expenses (but I recognise it won't grow in a straight line). If there is a high-risk/high-reward investment, I never see myself putting more than 1% into that opportunity. Oh, and if the whole world turns to chaos in some form of zombie apocalypse thing, I am pretty confident I can survive without the need for any money. A Japanese Samurai sword and my Decathlon running shoes should see me through that OK (and I am the grand master of being a tight arse when needed).

OTHER THINGS WHICH WILL HELP YOU ON YOUR JOURNEY.

The following are things that hopefully will help you navigate your career and overall outlook on things as they pertain to financial well-being. I hope they are relevant and make good sense:

1. Career hacks: Differentiate yourself.

CV and Interview Readiness:

Note a 'hack' isn't a shortcut - I just couldn't think of a better word to use.

OK, let's start this off with a bitch about school. I'm not sure about your experience, but as mentioned earlier, I don't recall ever getting any mentoring on what kind of career I could consider pursuing. At school, we had English, Math, Geography, Biology, Chemistry, Typing (yes, I am that old), Home Economics (sewing and cooking), Physical Education (PE), Woodwork, Engineering, Economics, and two languages you could choose (Maori and German). I guess the school concept is that you learn about them, and maybe you will find one super interesting, and that's the one you will follow, but even that wasn't explained to me. So, like most of us, we get to the end of high school (or not) and end up doing what sort of presents itself (as opposed to us pursuing it). That may be the right approach as in our early teenage years, we don't really give a shit about all that boring adult grown-up stuff (especially when we are focused on 'being cool' in front of our mates and especially in front of girlfriends or boyfriends). Unfortunately, what comes with this is that at some point, we do need to decide what to do work-wise or study-wise (Poly Techs/Apprenticeships/University).

The one big thing that puzzled me most (that the school overlooked) was when I went for my 1st interview (I had just turned 18). I had no training on how to write my CV, and that first interview was my first interview. Why didn't anyone coach me on interview skills, as some practice sessions would have been good?

This is really important because the biggest key factors when applying for a job are:

1: Getting an interview.

2: Getting the job.

And the best way to succeed at this is to **differentiate yourself.**

You never get true feedback when you don't pass an interview, as you never know exactly why it wasn't you. Of course, idiot brain will come up with lots of reasons/excuses.

Here are a few simple things to apply:

Spend time researching and making sure your CV is specific to the job you are applying for. If it's too general, then the employer will think, "They don't seem too bothered about this job."

Spend time doing interview practice sessions. Body language becomes key. And be prepared for them to ask, "What are your strengths and what are your weaknesses?" It's the weakness they are most interested in as this is designed as a "let's trip them up" question. My answer was always, "My weakness is I am quite impatient as I like things to be done right the first time, BUT it is something I am mindful of and pretty confident I can continue to work to find the correct balance." OK, in this example, I actually positioned my weakness into a strength without calling it out directly. Throughout my life, I have probably gone for a total of 10 interviews, and I have been offered about 7 of the jobs. I used to prepare well for them, with positive body language and just the right amount of confidence. I always made sure the interview was balanced. I was just as interested in finding out if this company/job was going to be the right fit for me as they were about me being the right fit for them. This is really important because the interviews became like a 2-way dialogue, and my asking relevant questions helped to differentiate me from the others. Spend time reviewing online some good interview habits – they make a big difference.

But before we even get to the interview process, how do I differentiate myself on my CV when I have zero work experience, my school grades were pretty average, and I went to a bit of a rough (perceived shit) school in the area. For me, this actually turned out to be luck rather than being planned. Big school or small school, get yourself engaged in some of the other programs they have going. Some examples I used:

We had a 1-week toastmaster (public speaking) session, which I signed up for. I got a certificate for this. I could put "certified introductory toastmaster" on my CV.

We had a couple of pretty basic school plays in which I played a very random part. If it's not your thing, then ask if you can take on some unimportant background role. Maybe you are the Christmas Tree. I could put on my CV "participated in 2 of the school play productions."

Sports: I represented our school in Rugby and Cricket (those are accurate, although we played cricket as a piss take). I represented the school in 100m hurdles. I was quite fast but not the fastest kid, but at our school, no one ever did the hurdles, so I entered that race because I knew it was my highest chance of winning a sport (too skinny for shot put), and we only had about 3 enter it and I won. Now, if you went to my school, you would think, 'Funny Wayne' because he won the 100m hurdles, and NO ONE does it. But if you didn't go to my school and were reviewing my CV and saw that

Wayne represented his school in 100m hurdles, you would think, "Oh, that's quite interesting." I also photo-bombed the table tennis photo (we made that one up on the day as we didn't have table tennis).

I could put on my CV "actively engaged in sport and represented the school in 1st XV rugby and 1st XI cricket and 100m hurdles and table tennis.

We had the annual school magazine, so I signed up to be part of that. My friend and I had a competition to see who could get our photos in the school magazine the most. I think we were both even as we photo-bombed as much as we could (before photo-bombing was a term)!

I could put on my CV "actively involved in the school magazine publication."

And I ended up as school head boy, which was a real boost... but part of me getting the head boy was "Wayne was actively involved in toastmasters, school play productions, rugby, cricket, athletics, table tennis and school magazine production and has used these platforms along with many others to display strong positive leadership skills."

When I went for my 1st interview, I was able to story tell, "Well, even though I high schooled in a bit of a rougher high school, I never let that hold me back from getting engaged and involved in extra activities: I didn't let the environment hold me back".

I was pretty confident that a kid from a bad reputation town of 5000 people and a school of only 600 students and marks between 50-70% would easily compete with a kid from a city of 100000 people and a school of 3000 students and marks much higher than mine: Reason = I could easily **differentiate** myself. So, as indicated above, this was mainly luck and just part of my natural character, but if you are at high school or University and want to differentiate yourself for that future interview (but don't want it to take up too much of your time) think of the little 'activity hacks' that may help you to differentiate yourself. Oh, and if they become really interesting, then you might enjoy them and learn lots from them.

Work for free?

If I was about to leave school and didn't know too specifically what I wanted to do, then I would draft a very good CV and send it with a cover letter (or hand deliver even better) to the biggest 10 companies in my area (nearest city): I am a big fan of working for large companies because they have many ladders to climb and therefore much more opportunity for growth than with a very small company. Opportunity for growth = reduced boredom and =s increased $$$ over time.

Dear Sir/Madam,

Thank you for taking the time to review my CV and my introductory letter. From my CV, you can see that in addition to achieving respectable exam results, I have also been actively engaged in many extra activities to help our school shine. I believe that, as a result, it has enabled me to develop some good natural leadership skills that will strongly benefit me and my future employer. I hope that my future employer will be Company XYZ.

I have been aware of Company XYZ since growing up due to the large positive presence in our community and your positive reputation for the overall work culture and work environment. As I am only 18, whilst I may be limited in my immediate work experience, I believe that by bringing my 'work hard' approach to Company XYZ along with your mentorship then, I can

quickly achieve the skills and experience so that we can grow together. Therefore, I would like to propose that I join Company XYZ as a junior management trainee for 1 year. During this 1-year period, I would be more than happy to work for FREE (no salary) as this will give me the environment to learn and develop and prove to Company XYZ that I can become a valuable future member of the management team. It might seem a little unusual for me to want to work for FREE, but I am confident that I can learn more practical skills in your environment in 1 year than I would learn in a 4-year University-related program. I am very effective at learning in a hands-on environment. I hope to get the opportunity to meet directly with your HR team and further present my credentials. Thank you very much for your time, and I hope to hear from you shortly.

Kind regards and thanks, Wayne.

OK, Wayne, you are **MAD, MAD, MAD!** Why work for free?

Here is the reality of the above:

- FREE? I have differentiated myself and, therefore, significantly increased my chances of getting an interview.
- I would learn more in 1 year (and not be adding debt) than 1 year in University. In the interview, I would highlight why University isn't a practical option due to family circumstances, but I would also highlight that if I can avoid debt, I can get my money working for me quicker. (Wow, this Wayne is really smart for his age when it comes to money stuff).
- As a management trainee, I would get exposure to many elements of the company and naturally find the best ladder to climb. Most large corporations can justify taking on a management trainee even if there is no specific headcount allocation for it.

- Of course, they are going to pay me. There is no way they will let me work for FREE. But if they insisted I work for FREE, then I would be fine with that.
- Out of 10 companies, I only need one to recruit me. In the worst case, I get no job, but I do get some interview experience and learn how to better differentiate myself.

Good idea? Or a stupid idea?

Non-Corporate Person:

If working for a large organisation isn't your thing, and going to University isn't your thing, and you don't really know what your thing is, then that can seem a bit daunting when starting out. If you do bumble into a job that might be for a small set-up (small owner business/retail/car repair/hairdressing, etc.), then I recommend you treat this as a job where you can discover yourself BUT also do an evening (or some form of online) course where you can learn the skills of basic accounting and how to run a small business. Maybe you like the work you have bumbled into, so set some goals for setting up your own business. Or maybe the owner loves the fact that you are ambitious and wants to mentor you so that one day you can take over the business. Opportunities always follow the person who demonstrates they are eager to develop and learn and have good work-hard, work-smart work ethics and integrity.

Gap Year/Backpacking:

You decide to take a year+ out of the career chase, but will this hold you back and make it difficult for you to find a job? That really depends on how you present yourself. I took a risk by taking 2.5 years out, but I had my sales pitch ready in case it was needed. "I am so glad I got that out of my system, and I can now really commit to my career. I learnt so much about myself on the road, especially when it comes to managing uncomfortable situations and navigating myself through different cultural nuances. This will really help me in team leadership roles. It's not easy managing the logistics of getting myself overland from China to Cyprus (without flying) on a super tight budget. These lessons will really help me in project management and the art of negotiation." No need to mention the naughty stuff you may have got up to!

Career Opportunist.

This following was quite defining for me in my career. Read more details about when I worked for Wang later on, but I was on a 6-week rolling contract in the UK when I was about 27 years old. A colleague and I were removed from a customer site as our company was perceived as having overpromised and underdelivered on a specific software solution to the customer. Nothing to do with my performance. So, in an open office environment in our London office, there were other employees who I got to know, and 2 interesting things happened.

1. They asked me once if I was concerned about job stability because I was on a 6-week rolling contract as they were full-time employees. My response was pretty much, "Nope, I am pretty confident that I can continue to show my value add to Wang, and if not, then I can

take this experience and use it with the next company I join. I am relevant, and I am employable."

2. Like a lot of employees, these guys would moan and bitch a lot about the company and the management style and the flaws in the way things were done. They would go to the pub for lunch (British culture) and moan and bitch a lot there too. I got on OK with them from a work perspective, and out of colleague politeness, but we were definitely on a different page about work ethics. Anyway, after a few weeks of listening to this, I asked to meet with their boss (not my boss, as I didn't really have one, as they were just keeping me around until this customer contract thing got sorted out). I knew Tina just through normal work politeness but had never had a work conversation with her. I asked her for a meeting as I had some ideas that might benefit her team. We had a closed-door meeting, and she was a little surprised when I asked her the following:

"Hi, Tina (the abridged version) – I understand from various communications that there are some current challenges with the following processes. I have been giving some thought to this, and as a straw man concept, I propose we improve the processes by reviewing and implementing the following changes. And I would love the chance to take the lead in implementing the changes. I have the bandwidth to do this, and confident Terry (my current kinda boss) would support this. Oh, and you don't need to worry about budget as my pay is covered by Customer XYX budget." She was a little taken aback by my approach, and we discussed things for a while. Two days later, she agreed that I should take the lead (which Terry was OK with). The moaning and bitching colleagues weren't that happy about it – but I was professional about it as I never name-called anyone out or threw anyone under the bus. We fixed things up as planned, and management and I were very happy.

This became the catalyst for me becoming the MR FIX IT person, and the range and scope of the assigned special projects continued to escalate in size and importance over the years. I became the Managing Director of our Singapore operations and Managing Director of our Greater China operations, as well as various senior regional roles, all focused on operational optimisation. I worked with Wang for about 11 years. Needless to say, the moaning and bitching colleagues were not with the company for much longer.

The key takeaways from this, which is super important in your working environment:

1. Don't be a moaner and bitcher. Come up with practical solutions to improve things positively. And many ladders will appear.

2. If you are not given the opportunity to improve things and you are confident you have approached this professionally, then you may find that this company is not the correct culture fit for you. That's OK, as it's better to learn early. When you look for a new company to work with, you can highlight that one of your frustrations is not being empowered to move things forward. This becomes a positive aspect of a new job interview.

3. NEVER lead with, I can fix this, but you have to pay me more. If you believe in yourself and the company culture, then the money will follow naturally. If you make it money lead, then you probably won't get the opportunity to implement the changes and grow with it.

4. You fixed the problem, and another problem and another problem, but the money hasn't followed. Then just have a conversation with those you need to talk to about this. But maybe this isn't the correct company culture to be with, and it is time for a change. And don't worry that you didn't get the extra money because you certainly got the extra experience which you take to your next employer.

5. You didn't get the Job Title you think you deserve! Is it that important? I got loads of things done and never worried much about the job title. People know how you fit within the hierarchy readily enough. People knew I had direct access to our International CEO and COO - it didn't matter that my title was Bid Manager.

6. Agility and flexibility are really important when in a work environment. You can read later when I moved from the UK to Hong Kong on the back of 3 days' notice. While you have no partner and kids, then super embrace this agility and flexibility as it is a differentiating asset that is easier to apply when young.

7. Always be professional. I was never a gossiper, and I would always apply the right amount of transparency needed. Quite a few times, I would get called up into the big meeting room upstairs and be surrounded by many people more senior than me, and I would be asked to give my opinion as I had been working on the project. I always found a way to navigate the conversation to ensure my viewpoint was expressed without pissing anyone off or without kissing anyone's bum. I am not a political player. I just knew how to communicate in a balanced manner. It used to be funny because the International CEO a couple of times would ask me to stay back and say, "Ah, I knew they were bullshitting me," and we would laugh about it.

When I was in my first year of work, I was enrolled in a programming course. After 3 sessions, I asked my manager if it would be OK if I didn't continue doing the course. I was concerned it was going to take me down a technical rabbit hole, which wasn't really where my strengths were. She was great and agreed that I didn't need to do the course anymore. I spent my whole work career in IT, and yet there is nothing tech about me. At various times, I had all sorts of subject matter experts reporting under me (permanent or on projects), such as Network consultants, Security consultants, Data Storage consultants, etc. I never bothered to learn much about the technical side of these things. What I did learn was what questions were required to find the best solution. A useful analogy is that we don't need Rolls-Royce parts to fix a Toyota. And the other key quality was I had a very good technical bullshit radar. Hard for a technical person not to overly technicalise a solution so I could work out quickly what was the right solution for the problem as opposed to the perfect solution for the problem.

Same thing with accounting. I have no accounting credentials at all, but you can put a P&L (profit and loss) statement in front of me, and I can quickly unravel that with a lot of questions (even when I don't have much knowledge of what the numbers represent). All I really look for are patterns and trends. "Why is this line showing a 30% increase compared to the last 5 years?" and I would focus on the numbers that make the biggest impact. No point spending half the review meeting on a $1000 over-budget when another line shows we are on a $1m over-budget!

Likewise, with client engagements. I am not a salesperson. Just not my style. I often got put on large customer projects that weren't going too well. Pretty quickly, I would assess what we weren't doing great and what the client wasn't doing great. I would then meet with the client and gauge if my assessment was correct, and if yes, then I would basically say to the customer, "If I can fix my things internally, then can you fix your things." Ultimately, it came down to did we both want things to work. Typically, we would find our middle ground, and things would improve very quickly. One customer refused to make any changes on their side, which was essentially saying they didn't want to work with us anymore, so I implemented an exit strategy from that customer. No point in bleeding with no solution in place.

We have an internal meeting, and I would volunteer to take the minutes even if I am chairing it. I would take my laptop and key the notes as the meeting was taking place. Typically, within 30 minutes of the meeting conclusion, I would send out the meeting minutes. I would clearly bullet point who had what action and by what date in the email body (and not in the attachments). Why was this important? Humans have short attention spans, and sending minutes requiring action 2 days later typically means momentum is lost. Sending minutes immediately has a pretty good knock-on effect of getting actions done quicker.

'Shit may hit the fan' management. Numerous times, I was praised for being straight up and honest in my work environment: no one likes surprises coming their way, and I was always good at providing an early "heads up there is an issue coming: these are the actions I am taking to resolve them. I got this covered. If I need your help, I will yell out, and I will keep you posted on the progress." This really helped as I now had senior management bought into working with me – and even when something did turn to shit, it was shit they had on their radar: much easier to deal with and manage.

This is not my career-related, but I have had a few meetings (friends of friends) with people looking to open a small business. My first request, of course, is to please present to me your 3-year business plan. I want to see how your business will differentiate itself and also the financial details on your cost of set up, operational costs, revenue projection, trigger points where you may expand the business, projected profit margins, and most importantly, your cash burn (when do you run out of cash). I once had a conversation similar to the following:

Them: I don't have any of those details.

Wayne: How do you know your business will be profitable?

Them: Well, the pharmacy across the road seems to be making good money.

Wayne: You are shitting me!! That's the basis of your investment thesis"?

(Within a 3km radius of where I live, there are over 10 pharmacies. Boots franchise just opened a new pharmacy right next door to an existing small pharmacy. That's just stupid!!)

Oh, and I don't recommend getting tattoos that are visible above your collar line/sleeve line. If you love tattoos, that's cool. Just make sure they are not visible when going for a job interview. Some interviewers may be prejudiced against tattoos. Why limit potential career options for the sake of a few centimetres extra of ink? And if you are not looking for an office environment job and think tattoos won't matter so much, well, maybe at 18 you are a building apprentice, but then maybe you discover you are really good at construction and love property and then find you really want to take your knowledge and become a design architect or even sell real estate. Oops, now you are in office, and these neckline tattoos may hold you back. It's important to learn how to 'walk the line' to ensure you are relevant even if you don't 100% agree with the line you are required to walk: small compromise = more opportunity? "Don't shoot yourself in the foot" is an old cliche that sums this up quite well. Maybe get those few extra centimetres of ink when you get your Financial Freedom as a way to celebrate. So, I guess when we say Differentiate, we are saying Positively Differentiate.

You may recall a few years back that, getting ear lobe discs was a little bit popular. Well, they aren't so popular now. I see a few droopy hanging empty ear lobes in Thailand. I wonder if they regret that youthful decision or not.

In summary regarding career hacks: keep **differentiating yourself**. That aligns to keep challenging yourself. The reward for this is pretty simple: Increased $$$ = Increased savings = Increased $$$ plugged into your Financial Freedom plan = Financial Freedom achieved earlier.

2. What can we blame the Government for?

Just a quick blurb on a recurring theme I see more and more, and that is the unhealthy ongoing blaming of the Government. This is going to vary significantly depending on where you are from and where you are living. We don't have the perfect Government anywhere, and some are really bad (corruption is the worst), but regardless, try to minimise how much you keep blaming the Government for everything. You can make changes by getting involved or simply by voting. But you should always take a step back and ask yourself how you navigate your way forward financially, even with a Government you may not like or feel doesn't provide an environment for you to achieve your goals. Better to say, "stuff it, I will make this work for me regardless" (assuming you don't move forward in a corrupt and dishonest fashion). Ties back into positive thinking, don't play victim and self-motivation. There is always a way to get ahead of the bunch.

In the 80s growing up I recall so many people in NZ complaining about the Government. In 2024, I often hear people saying how lucky we were back in the 80s due to house pricing affordability, etc. Hmmm, but at the time, the NZ Government was shit??? In summary (to a certain % of the population), the Government always has been and always will be shit. Don't get held back in that rhetoric and navigate your way forward positively.

Presently, there is a bit of media coverage about how the cost of property affordability versus the average wage in places like NZ, Australia, Canada, the UK, etc., has never been worse and therefore, the 70s and 80s were the lucky generation. Maybe or maybe not? I shared a flat from the age of 18 to about 32 as a way to save money, as renting a whole house seemed really expensive, and buying one seemed really expensive, too. None of my friends even thought of buying their own house in their 20s to live in. And, of course, interest rates on the property back in the 70s and 80s ranged at times above 10 to 17%, but that never gets a mention. Don't get caught up or held back in the negative hype. Look at the data and use that to assist with your own narrative and navigate a way through it that's financially beneficial to you.

And boy, I hate it when I hear that growing up in the 70s and 80s were the best times ever. Well, that depends on where you grew up, what your race is, what your sexual preference is, etc. It normally reflects back to kids climbing trees and not being glued to phones and listening to cool rock bands. But I am pretty sure this has nothing to do with the 70s and 80s, but it has everything to do with those early teenage years to about 25. Those years typically will always be the best because those are the years where you form the best memories. Probably about 90% of the music I listen to is from the 1980s. That's probably the same with most of my school friends. Those born in 1977 likely listen mainly to music in the 90s. What a coincidence! In 2080, will the 'old gen' be saying, "Wow, so glad I grew up in the 2030s when we only had 7g, and we didn't have all of these semiconductor chips inserted in us."

3. Chasing the money = Yep, it is a game.

Be prepared that when you do reach your Financial Freedom goals, you will continue to chase the money. It's just wired into probably all of us to want more $$$ (we are capitalist pigs!!) I have a school friend who also retired early and is also a bit of a tight arse like me. We both have enough money to get us easily to our finish line. When we catch up, we do laugh at ourselves about our desire to continue to grow our net worth to a point where it is a crazy amount that we would never spend, and we think that's OK because we recognise we are playing the game. But we also recognise that this desire to increase our net worth will not be at the expense of us becoming greedy and taking stupid, unnecessary risks. Yep, it's a game, but we have our own clear boundaries within which we operate. That makes it fun to see how it will turn out!

4. Post-retirement challenges.

OK, you are about to retire – congratulations. Let's assume you have the Financial Freedom breathing space, so we won't make this section about the $$$ side of things as that's all pretty well covered above by basic money behaviours. The challenge is how to make your retirement fulfilling and not boring. I have met quite a few who continue to work even though they can afford to retire, and that's great, BUT please don't complain about your job and the stress it brings you. I used to run with a guy who still worked (and I didn't), and he would moan and bitch about his work, but I had to ask him to not moan and bitch about it in front of me – he had options not to work, but he continued to work – not to attain Financial Freedom but more because he didn't have a plan. I have asked quite a few people in their early 50s when they expect to retire, and they don't know – they don't have a plan.

If I ask people how they plan to spend their retirement, I normally get broad answers, and the most common is to travel. So, I ask them where they would like to travel and how often, and I tend to get vague answers. One 57-year-old lady can't wait until retirement, and I asked her what she wants to do, and she said work in her backyard garden: that's great if that's her thing, but I was kind of expecting something a bit more than that.

Perhaps the most common theme for those who don't have a real plan is they don't have **active hobbies**. They may have left them behind when they had kids or feel they are now 'too old' to have active hobbies. Well, there are so many 70s+ people who still ride bicycles (maybe an e-bike) or do hiking or golf or tennis or padel or pickleball or.......... If you are a bit out of shape, well, that's an awesome retirement challenge – take up walking (or rucking = walking with weights) and use the new spare time/routine to change to a healthier diet. Please use your imagination = **it's not that hard!**

Some people work a lot longer than they need to (plan or no plan) because their work defines them. I once met a guy in a condo gym, and it went something like this:

Wayne: Hi, I'm Wayne.

Him: Hi, I am Dr John.

Wayne: You mean John?

Him: Yes, Dr John.

Wayne: But you are not my doctor, so I will just call you John if that's OK?

Him: Yes, that's OK.

This leads to an interesting exercise: You meet a stranger, and you ask them, "Nice to meet you. Please tell me 5 things about yourself." If they lead with, "Oh, I work as a this or a that at this company", then they most likely are too defined by their work and not by who they are as a person!

Military Personnel: OK, U.S readers, please **don't shoot me** on this one because you guys are very patriotic to your veterans compared to most other countries, but I always find it strange when I see a serviceman's (or ex-serviceman's gravestone) and especially those who didn't die in battle and their headstone reads "Lance Corporal Pat Patterson." Why? In civilian life, we don't see a headstone that reads "Postman Pat Patterson" or "Forklift Driver Pat Patterson." (My dad died 35 years after he retired from the army, and he had his military rank put on his cemetery plaque. I thought that was weird)!

Most people retire around 65, and by default, it is less difficult to work out how to spend your day/weeks/years because they typically think they will only be health-wise active until about 75ish, and then they need to consider slowing down. So, their typical plan is to travel and do kids/grandkids type stuff. But 65 to 90 is still 25 years, so it

156

would be cool to have a clearer plan than just letting that time drift by.

Retiring early, like 45, poses some different challenges because that is 45 years to plan for, and you hopefully have very good health still. My approach to early retirement was to find something I am super passionate about and that will help keep me busy and active. The reality is I have lots of things I like doing but nothing I am super passionate about. Fortunately, I do like to stay active, and typically, when I am in Thailand, my day is a mix of running, cycling, hiking, and tennis. I try and do 2 outdoor activities per day. So that's great for the body but not for the mind (unless I keep the score in tennis). One of my concerns is that if I don't keep my brain active, then maybe I will get Alzheimer's or Dementia at a younger age. I also got a few head knocks from my rugby days - Yikes! So, I manage that by reading (80% non-fiction), and I spend about an hour each day checking in on my stock/ETF portfolio and the markets, etc. It's a fun hobby; it keeps me relevant, and my Excel brain keeps working.

I typically travel 8 to 12 weeks a year, so time goes into planning that and, of course, once on the road that keeps all the senses engaged. As yet, I haven't bothered with volunteer work because I am the sort of person who, if I get involved, I want to ensure it is done right – and with that, I will tend to put extra responsibility on myself. I love having very little responsibility cause that, to me, is the awesome part of the Freedom equation. When I was still living in Singapore, I used to run my 12km loop along the river/Marina Bay. I used to love watching all 'the suits' going to work and me not going to work – having those mornings free to myself is still priceless after 13+ years. I don't really plan on slowing down either - I assume I will be running and riding and playing tennis into my late 80s and quite look forward to the challenges that will present.

While I don't look forward to slowing down with age, I am looking forward to seeing how well I can maintain my activity levels with age. Until what age can I run 10 km? I can't wait (yes, I can) to find that one out.

My biggest challenge I face with early retirement (or even late retirement) will likely be boredom, and if that's my biggest challenge, then you will never hear me complain because that boredom is up to me, and that's a very cool problem and challenge to have to tackle.

So to summarise, have a retirement **plan** that keeps you active, healthy, mentally stimulated and challenged. Ikigai (Japanese concept of long living) includes community/social types of engagement too.

5. CIGARETTES: Yuk puke and the worst money burner ever:

OK, caveat on this one first. I have never smoked a cigarette in my life. Tried one when I was probably 12, but after 2 puffs, I knew I would never take a 3rd. I tried some weed when I was about 14, but after 3 puffs, I knew I would never take a 4th. My dad smoked a pipe: yuk puke. He used to tell himself (and us) that smoking a pipe was a lot healthier than smoking cigarettes – as if that gave him a free pass. He would smoke it in the house, and he always stunk of pipe smoke. And he had a very yellow thumb from years of pushing his tobacco into his pipe. But rather than rant and rave about smoking, here's what, from an investment perspective, I will focus on.

Smoking is literally watching your money go up in smoke. Yep, we know that! Tell us something new!

I sometimes see on YouTube people on the benefits complaining about how tough it is to move forward financially, and often, they are smoking a ciggie and that got me thinking about what the opportunity investment cost of smoking is. So, I ran some quick numbers as follows: (I will run the NZ example first but will follow up with other major countries as well)

In New Zealand, in August 2024, the cost of a packet (20) of cigarettes cost NZD40.

Start smoking from 20 years old to 65 years old.

Smoke 1 packet per week

1 x 52 x \$40 = \$2080/year

X 45 years = \$93600 up in smoke.

(Note: smokers seem to smoke about 10 cigarettes per day, so that would turn out as 3.5 packs/week so that it would become:

3.5 x 52 x \$40 = 7289/year

X 45 years = $327600 up in smoke.

Note that the above numbers assume no inflation, and the cost of cigarettes remains at $40 forever.

That's a lot of money up in smoke, but hey, maybe you have a big ego and say, "stuff it, over the period of 45 years, I can afford to burn from $90k to $330k, and so I am going to keep on smoking."

But what if, instead of smoking every year, you invested the $2080 into a U.S. index tracker fund (the S&P 500 SPLG ETF)? Historically, this has returned > 10% per year for the past 100 years. Do you find this investment too risky??? Well, it's not as risky as smoking, so we will go with this.

Based on 1 packet per week @ $40 at 45 years at 10% interest reinvested (compounded each year) starting at 20 and ending at 65years old, the opportunity cost of your smoking has gone from $93600 to **$1.811 million up in smoke**: I hope this number is enough to say stuff my ego and stuff smoking.

Oh, and if you were a 3.5 pack per week smoker, then the $327,600 now compounding at 10% jumps to a staggering **$ 6.3 million up in smoke:** YIKES. (again, assuming no inflation).

If I was the NZ Government and serious about ending smoking, I wouldn't bother with the lung cancer pictures on packaging as it seems smokers have become immune to that. I would simply billboard and packet advertise: **"A packet a week will cost you $1.8m, so don't be a DICK – oh, and you will probably die younger too!!**

And if you counter-argue that Governments will lose all the tax from cigarettes, well, yes, that is true, but then Governments will spend less on medical care too, so maybe swings and roundabouts on taxes collected versus tax money spent. OK, but 'no smoking' should equal a longer life until death, so that will mean the Governments will spend more on looking after the elderly. Well, maybe if the money was now being invested instead of smoked, the elderly would be better positioned to know how to look after themselves financially.

Below are the spreadsheet details of the NZ cost of smoking, but if you think well, NZ is the most expensive country in the world to smoke (don't forget NZ does have free healthcare, so if you get ill from smoking, at least that part is free) so it doesn't apply to me then the following chart shows the cost and opportunity cost for a few other countries too. I would love to get in a debate with anyone who can justify this waste of money and lost opportunity in getting to Financial Freedom:

Note I have grouped NZ and Australia together as there isn't much cost difference.

In local country currency.	NZ/Australia	Canada	U.S
Cost: Packet of 20 cigarettes	$40.00	$12.50	$6.50
Packets smoked per week	1	1	1
Packets smoked per year	52	52	52
Cigarette spend per year	$2,080	$650	$338
Total spent over 45 years of smoking	$95,680	$29,900	$15,548
Opportunity cost at 10% compounding	$1,811,628	$566,134	$294,390

	NZ/Australia	Canada	U.S
Packets smoked per week	3.5	3.5	3.5
Total spent over 45 years of smoking	$334,880	$104,650	$54,418
Opportunity cost at 10% compounding	$6,340,697	$1,981,468	$1,030,363

In local country currency.	UK	Germany	Singapore
Cost: Packet of 20 cigarettes	£12.60	€ 7.00	$14.87
Packets smoked per week	1	1	1
Packets smoked per year	52	52	52
Cigarette spend per year	£655	£364	$773
Total spent over 45 years of smoking	£30,139	£16,744	$35,569
Opportunity cost at 10% compounding	£570,663	£317,035	$673,473

	UK	Germany	Singapore
Packets smoked per week	3.5	3.5	3.5
Total spent over 45 years of smoking	$105,487	$58,604	$124,492
Opportunity cost at 10% compounding	$1,997,320	$1,109,622	$2,357,154

The maths: with ciggie savings compounding each year at 10% return in NZD/AUD.

Packet of 20 ciggies	$40
Packets per week	1
Packets per year	52
Total/yr on ciggies	$2,080

Compounding interest with savings added each year

AGE	$/year		Interest	Gain	$$ value	No Comp'ding
20	$2,080		10%	$208	$2,288	
25	$2,080	$16,048	10%	$1,605	$17,653	12,480
30	$2,080	$38,545	10%	$3,854	$42,399	22,880
35	$2,080	$74,775	10%	$7,478	$82,253	33,280
40	$2,080	$133,125	10%	$13,313	$146,438	43,680
45	$2,080	$227,098	10%	$22,710	$249,808	54,080
50	$2,080	$378,442	10%	$37,844	$416,287	64,480
55	$2,080	$622,184	10%	$62,218	$684,402	74,880
60	$2,080	$1,014,732	10%	$101,473	$1,116,205	85,280
65	$2,080	$1,646,934	10%	$164,693	$1,811,628	95,680

Note the column on the right shows no compounding. i.e., the money saved from smoking is not reinvested.

I trimmed the rows for each year for formatting purposes.

The key takeaway from above: If you do smoke, then please **QUIT** and put that money (which you were going to burn up anyway) and invest it every year (or more frequently) into an S&P500 index tracker ETF. If you don't smoke, then don't start (and hopefully, you don't get into vaping either).

And smoking cannabis **is** still smoking – but probably more expensive – and certainly don't smoke 3 packs per week.

And please don't smoke a pipe yuk!

OK – to keep it simple DON'T SMOKE anything.

6. The Coffee Fix: and other similar habits.

OK, clearly not as dangerous for your health as smoking, but it's still a very expensive 'lost investment opportunity.' If the average branded coffee is USD3.50 and you drink 1 per day, then it's roughly USD1300/year. Over 45 years, that is USD58600 spent on branded coffee. If you invested USD1300/year in the S&P500 at 10%, then over 45 years compounding, that is USD1.1 million equivalent.

So, just how much do you love your coffee now??

Running bad spending habits through the compounding calculator is a really good way to talk yourself out of unnecessary habitual spending. Remember, looking at numbers in a spreadsheet can help remove emotion from the uncomfortable decision-making process. Remember this image?

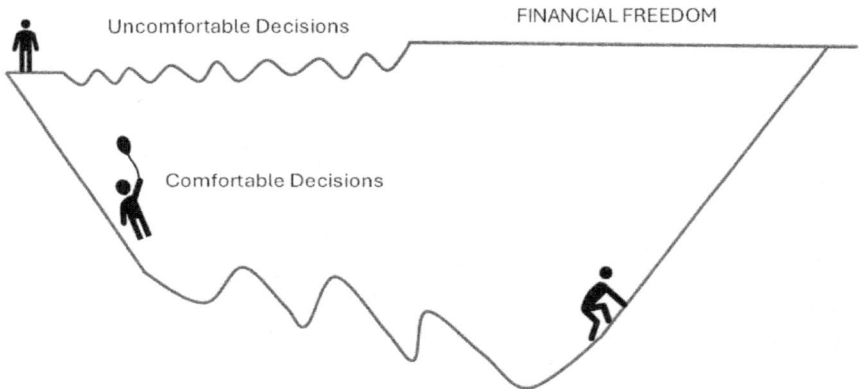

I don't drink hot drinks. I worked out when I was a kid that if I drank a hot coffee or tea, Mum would ask me to make them and also make me clean the cups. The easiest way to get out of that was to simply stop drinking them. Problem solved!

7. More about me – if you aren't sick of me by now!

(you can skip this part, and you won't hurt my feelings).

OK, I feel as if I rambled on a bit too much about myself already in the above. Apologies for that. It wasn't my intention, but I found it hard not to include actual first-hand experiences. Below will hopefully provide some other examples of how I took action as opportunities came my way – finding the balance between managing one's comfort zone is key to moving forward financially. I won't cover details on my personal partner relationships – for privacy reasons – sorry, no juicy gossip!!

Oddly, this has pretty much turned into a mini autobiography: Weird! Sorry!!

It's a little longer than 162 words, but hopefully, you can find some relatable elements in my journey to your own.

SWEEEEET, SWEETS, SWEETIE, SPEEDY, and BUCK SWEET, are various nicknames I can recall. My favourite is still SWEETIE because I love the weird looks my male mates sometimes get when calling me that. In Asia, it's sometimes difficult for "Wayne" to be pronounced, so that often gets called "Way Neee," which is fun. SWEET has been a very fun surname.

Born in New Zealand in 1967, the youngest of 7 boys (13-year age gap). I grew up in a fairly tense/angry household. Back in the day, when smacking kids and calling them little shits was the social norm, I guess. I could never work out why my mum, who was very non-religious, called all her 7 sons Jesus 'bloody' Christ all the time – it was confusing growing up!

Dad was working his way up the ranks in the army, and Mum was a housewife. Mum died of cancer when I just turned 17. Dad remarried when I was 17 and 3 months old. At this point, I recognise

I am on my own, so it's a battle through shit family life/last year of school until I get to 18, then I get my first job. **Freeeee** at last...

As Dad was in the army, we moved around a bit, so I got used to "catch ya later" moments, knowing I would never see my best friends again (no social media back then), but I thought that was just the norm, so no big deal. When I was 11-13, though, I was super lucky because Dad got a posting to Singapore (NZ used to have an army base/Australia had an air force base), and 5 of us (4 oldest had left home) had a totally new experience. Singapore was for sure my most fun growing up years. It was the first time Mum seemed really happy, and as kids, we could run riot, and no one seemed to care. It's cool that I ended up back in Singapore (Love You Singapore) later for my career, and maybe those 2 years as a kid is why I really connect to living in Southeast Asia.

Back in NZ, I was pretty lucky to be in the same high school from age 13.5 to 18 years old. I was in a pretty small high school (about 600 kids), and we certainly had a reputation as being rough and low achieving (low decile school, I think, is the more common reference these days). Ngaruawahia is not known as the flashiest place to live in NZ. I have no idea if we had great teachers or not because I only went to one high school, so I can't compare them. I did get the cane once – oh, the good old days! We had a large freezing works (abattoir) up the road, and quite a few kids left at 16 to go and work there. The $/hr. was pretty decent at the time, so it was an easy choice for most, BUT as kids/parents, no one was really looking longer term. In our last year, we only had about 10 of us left - so many had left, which I thought at the time was unfortunate. You get a good $/hr at 16, but what will it be like when you are 20, 25, or 30? I was always locked into being ok with a lower wage if it meant it would ramp up quickly as I got older. I enjoyed school as it was great to get away from home. I was never bullied. I think I may have been a verbal (not physical) bully when I was a kid, and if that's the case, I apologise for that. I certainly readily take a stand against bullies these days. Amongst my mates - I was known to win all my fights by 50 metres. Oddly, to this day, I have never been in a big punch-up or been beaten up (or beaten anyone up). I have been in quite a few tense situations, including having the odd knife pulled on me (about 3 times when travelling Turkey/Turkiye back in the 90s of all places – Turkiye is awesome), but have always managed to either calm the situation down OR acted so ballistically crazy that the person(s) have backed off. Once near the border town in Turkiye and Iran, someone jumped out in the early evening with a knife and tried to rob me and my friend. I calmly said, "Ohhh piss off, will ya?" we didn't even break our walk stride, so we basically just ignored him. It was super funny when we looked back, and he was holding his knife and wondering what had just happened. I have lots of other funny stories like this, but that's a different book, maybe!

Academically, I passed my exams, but I would range in the 50 to 70% pass rate, so not super academic. I stuffed around in class a lot as I enjoyed being the funny kid to make others laugh, so many didn't think I was too serious. But when I was at home I was quite studious with my homework and study– it gave me a quiet place.

In my last year of school, I was appointed Head Boy (prefect). I guess someone saw that I had potential leadership qualities, and this helped me get a job easily enough.

I got a job working at a plastic bag manufacturer for 4 years, starting as a computer trainee. This was before we realised what horrible things to the environment plastic bags would become. I quite liked working and learning new stuff hands-on. It was pretty much a 9 to 5 type of work, but I was always happy to volunteer to do anything in the early evening. After 4 years, I was getting itchy feet and needed a change. I went to 3 interviews, and one of them said, "We would really like to get you on board, but we can't justify matching your current salary because of your age." What the heck does my age have to do with my value to the company?? To get a job with more scope, I needed to move from Hamilton (about 100k people) to Auckland (about 1m people and 140km away). I didn't really know anyone in Auckland. An English guy who I knew said, "Why don't you go to London – you can earn stg10/hr there." Hmm, well I don't know anyone in London - but then I don't know anyone in Auckland either – so I decided I would head to the UK for a 2-year OE (overseas experience). Aussie and Kiwis could work in the UK back then (maybe still can today) on a 2-year work visa. 2 years was my goal - I left NZ in 1990. 34 years later, I kinda miscalculated that one.

I was lucky as the plastic bag company I worked for in NZ had a manufacturing subsidiary in Telford, The Midlands, UK, and I had arranged to work for them for 2 weeks doing some training for them.

Well, I got lucky cause during the 2 weeks, they liked me, and we negotiated a 6-month contract as I helped them optimise the use of the manufacturing software they were using (as it was originally from NZ). I had a day rate way better than I was on in NZ, and they gave me a company car. Telford was an affordable place to live, and the NZD to the Sterling was 3:1 (these days, it's about 2:1), so I was very focused on saving those Sterlings.

Cultural funny: Almost everyone uses the word 'bugger' in NZ and Australia, and its literal meaning is really gross. However, for some reason it's just a normal word that is even used on TV adverts a bit. When I started working in Telford I was politely asked by my manager to stop using that word. Bugger me, it was really hard not saying the word Bugger – but I did adjust = I just swapped the word Bugger for Budgie. "Budgie Me' is still a bit gross, though.

After that, I moved to London, and I got a job working for a large tea manufacturer as their Systems Analyst. It was a full-time job, and the money was not as good as the contract I was on, but I figured I could climb the ladder easily enough. The job turned out to be a bit boring as it wasn't as much IT project-related stuff and more me helping out with the tea factory planning. But that was OK cause I was really enjoying living in London as I flatted in a 4 bedroom house with about 8 others (Aussies and Kiwis) so my costs were low and it was great to get out and explore the UK and some cool parts of Europe (the Munich Beerfest and the Pamplona running of the bulls in Spain were two standout trips). So that year went pretty quickly, and I started to get itchy travel feet, which was a bit of a first.

In February 1992, I decided I would try to travel from Greece to South Africa overland for 1 year, and a flatmate came as far as Turkiye with me. The short version of this is I couldn't overland it all as Sudan was in the civil war (fancy that as they are back at it again), so I zig-zagged Greece, Turkiye, Syria, Jordan, Israel, Egypt (flew to Kenya) and then Uganda, Zaire, Tanzania, Malawi, Zambia, Zimbabwe and finally South Africa. I flew back to the UK after about 13 months on the road, and I hardly spent any money. It was pre-internet, and it was amazing how many times I got free accommodation at hostels simply by asking, "If I stay for a few days for free food and accommodation, I think I can help to find you more guests." Hitch-hiking was cheap, too!

I got back to the UK, and I only had about 6 months left on my UK work visa, but I figured I would find a decent-paying job for that time. But I ended up back in my old flat in London, and it was kind of crap weather, and this Aussie guy dossing on the floor in the lounge with me was pretty keen to try and do London to Australia overland – no flying.

April 1993. Without any plans, we set off. We did the UK, France, Germany, Czechoslovakia, Hungary, Romania, Bulgaria, Turkiye (we did that super quick with a bit of hitchhiking as it was relatively expensive for our budget), then Turkiye, Iran, Pakistan, India, Nepal, India, Bangladesh and arrrggghhhh we couldn't get thru Myanmar back then and we couldn't overland back to Pakistan, China and cross into Vietnam back then either so we flew to Bangkok from Calcutta (Kolkata now). I arrived in Thailand for the 1st time in Oct 1993, and my friend headed south towards Australia (I never saw him again, so I had no idea how he got on), and I flew to Hong Kong with the plan of overlanding back to the UK from there. I flew to Taiwan to try to teach English, but they wanted an MTV American-style accent, and I have a really flat-sounding Kiwi accent. They didn't want my 'Tracta/Docta' when they were looking for a 'Tracterr/Docterr' accent. So back to HK for 2 months (taught some English at the HK Jockey Club) and then to China, Russia (trans-Siberian train), Estonia, Sweden, Germany, Netherlands and the UK.

This was about a 13-month trip, and I was only out of pocket around USD1k. Life was cheaper back then but I also had some pretty interesting sleeping outside experiences.

I spent about 2 years and 3 months on the road and was looking forward to a few months of work routine in the UK before planning to head off to South America. Career can wait – as the cost of life on the road wasn't much: just the opportunity cost of not earning decent money was getting skipped.

Those travel years are totally jam-packed with weird adventures and life experiences, which I kept in a diary. Great education and beats listening to some geography teacher at the front throwing chalk at me. Fortunately, I still like to get out on the road and have mini adventures, and I still like to kinda old school travel (OK, I have a phone and internet and maps.me and eBooks), but not much else has changed about my travel style over the years.

I got back to the UK. It's May 1994, and I am 27. I phoned up someone I knew from NZ who is now in the UK delivering a contract to Wang Computers as he specialised in the same NZ manufacturing software, and wow, I got a 10-day contract and I can start in 2 days. Super because in 10 days I earned the same amount as the money I spent on the last 13 months travelling. Life was cool.

But again, during my 10 days, it seemed they really liked me and asked if I could stay on longer, so I signed up for a 6-week auto-renewing contract. I had some maybe visa issues looming, so I thought I would find out exactly where my grandparents were born. And turns out my mum's dad was actually born in the UK and left when he was about 10. That let me apply for a 4-year ancestor visa - which I got: shit, was I lucky. I am now earning good money again, living in a house with 5-8 others and really enjoying the 'corporate routine.' Only a big problem is looming – the main customer using this manufacturing software is really pissed with Wang and wants to throw everyone off-site and start the process of totally disengaging from the contract. I was commuting from London to Doncaster once a week, and the customer asked everyone to be kicked off-site except for me. That was weird but good for me and my reputation with Wang. The contract terminated after a few months, but Wang needed to keep me on because they were some possible legal proceedings, and I would be able to help with that because of my knowledge. I was back in the London office with 1 other colleague from the same contract, but we didn't have too much to do. He messed around in the office, being a bit of a lazy bum and laughing that he was still getting paid. I took a different route! On our floor was a team working on submitting international bids to win big new business. I knew nothing about this, BUT that didn't stop me from walking over to the manager (who I now knew) and saying, "Hi - I am pretty much doing nothing here all day, but they need to keep me for a short while. While I am doing nothing, how about I do something, and I will do that something for you? You can assign me whatever work you want, and I will do my best to get it done. My costs won't impact your budget, so essentially, I am free labour for you." After a couple of quick calls and yippee, I am assigned to work on her team as well. After about 3 weeks, the other guy gets terminated, and I am as busy as ever on my 6-week rolling contract. It didn't take long until I built a strong reputation as the guy who gets shit done, and he is happy to get shit done late into the evening too. Reference career hack earlier in this section.

The short version is that I proved my worth in the Bid Management Team and implemented new and improved processes. Wang kept throwing all sorts of new projects for me to work on. It used to be quite funny cause, technically, I reported to one person, but I did about 80% of my work for others. A typical scenario:

"Wayne, do you know anything about optimising logistics?"

Me: "No"

"Wayne, can you go to Belgium for 2 weeks to sort out some major issues with Logistics overspending?"

Me: "Yes"

And so off I go. The guy running the show there was a South African guy, and so rather than him seeing me as a threat, I was pretty straight up and said we got to work through this stuff together, and I will be very transparent about what I find. We worked super well together, and within 4 weeks, we collectively proposed some changes, which ripped out about $1m of cost savings.

More projects like this kept coming my way. Super enjoyed it.

I had a direct line by then to the International CEO and COO. They tried to get me off my 6-week rolling contract a few times (they had bumped the rate up a few times, but the best part was I got time+ for anything over 37 hours/week), and this is where I made my best killing. If you need someone to work late on this, I can do it. I was always putting my hand up for overtime overtime overtime, and they didn't care if they paid me more because I would fix the problem. I never told any other colleagues about my overtime arrangement – they didn't need to know. I wouldn't go full-time because I set up an offshore company through the Isle of Man, so I had a tax advantage, and I would say if you want me to give up the contract and go permanent, then please ensure my net $$ in my hand is the same as my current set up. I assured them I wasn't going anywhere as they were really good at looking after me, and I was really good at looking after them.

This was going great, and I was enjoying all the special projects they were sending me on around Europe and Asia. I let them know I really enjoyed working on the Asia projects.

Then, a very cool thing happened. Wang was acquiring an old Italian company called Olivetti.

Thursday early afternoon, I get called up by the international CEO and COO for a meeting. Just me and them. (my current boss wasn't invited).

"Wayne, we need you to take on a new role in Asia, taking the lead in 'bid management and operations."

Me – OK. Which country will I be based in?

"Wayne, we think Hong Kong, but maybe Singapore:

Me – OK. Hong Kong is cool. When do you want me to start?

"Wayne, can you start on Monday"?

Me – OK. What about my 6-week contract?

"Wayne, you will need to go permanent. We don't know the exact details but don't worry. We will ensure you are financially better off."

Me – OK, sounds cool.

After a quick handshake and pats on the back, I packed up everything that evening and flew to Hong Kong on Saturday. I show up in the office on Monday. Catch up with the Head of Asia Pacific (who I had done some work with before), and we work out my scope of work (and my title), and we get on with stuff.

And yes, they sorted out my package as they promised.

August 1998: Asia begins. Hong Kong: It was pretty funny as we had to sort out the old Olivetti 'mafia' style of big expats in big chairs in Singapore, Malaysia, Japan, South Korea, etc. I was only 31 at the time, so these older guys didn't really see me as any form of threat and would quite happily share their egocentric "why they are so important' blah blah blah to me." I loved it because I would then have a quick session with my boss (British guy, probably about 60), and we would agree on a very quick "get them the hell out of the company" strategy. We tidied things up very quickly.

After 2 years in HK, I relocated to Singapore. We were acquired by a Dutch IT company called Getronics. They didn't have a direct presence in Asia, so we didn't have any culling to do, and being from NZ, I was very fortunate as the Dutch are even more straight up than Kiwi culture, so I got on really well with the new style.

At age 33, I ended up being Managing Director of Singapore (we had about 300 employees), and it was struggling with cashflow/profit/growth and I turned that around really quickly. But I know my strengths and weaknesses, which is really important. I told management once I had it turned around, I was not the best person to grow it from there. I actively looked for the right person (internally) who took over from me within about 18 months. I then moved back to HK and took on the role of Managing Director of Greater China and kind of did the same thing again. Then, after 2 years back to a regional role in Singapore. Getronics was struggling globally by this time, and by default, I became the 'cost cutter' guy in Asia, so we closed down the South Korea operations, scaled back Japan, etc. I was good at cost-cutting and retaining operational effectiveness, but that wasn't the most motivating role.

Plus, I was faced with a more important challenge: and that was simply lifestyle balance burnout. When you work for a global company in a regional role and have some global responsibilities, and you have a large U.S. presence, then simply by time zone, you end up on a lot of evening conference calls. It wasn't unusual to be in the office from 0815 to 1845. A quick meal and then get on a conference call from 2100 to 2200+, and maybe I was doing this 2 to 3 evenings a week. If I was not on a conference call, then I was maybe flying to/from somewhere in the evenings and at weekends. I was getting burnt out/frustrated with a company not really going forward. But there was something else really pulling at me too... and that was I had the 'Financial Freedom finishing line" getting nearer and nearer, and it's amazing how that plays with the brain and says, "Do you really need to be putting up with this shit." After 13 years with Wang/Getronics, I decided to semi-retire (Aged 40). I was super grateful to have worked for these guys – it suited my style really well, and I don't ever recall getting caught up in the political bullshit game – maybe that's thanks to the company, or maybe that's thanks to my own style.

From a cultural perspective, I think I was good at managing that. Maybe it was my 2.5 years of backpacking. We have many subtle nuances in the different Asian countries, and it's important to be aware of them. No good, just being the EXPAT blah blah my way or the highway style. Here is a good example: When I would hold a regional workshop with colleagues from all around the Asia Pacific, I would take the Australian colleagues aside and let them know - "I am going to kick this regional meeting with some questions designed to promote a lot of engaging discussions - please do not jump in and take the floor by answering all the questions first – please just sit back a while and let the rest of the other country teams contribute first." The reason was very simple: When English isn't your first language, and you have a super respectful culture (e.g. Japan), it can create a shy environment when thrust together with strangers. But once the ice is broken by them leading first, then it creates effective team engagement. Fortunately, the Australian colleagues were very supportive.

At 40, I figured it was time to take an extended break. I considered it officially semi-retired but I had no idea how much the semi-hours in a week would entail. I was relocating to Bali as I had bought a villa there as my new home. I did ship a 'container of furniture to Australia project,' but that was basically too much work for not much return, so it wasn't worth the hassle. Then, after 6 months of stuffing around, an ex-colleague said they needed help at one of the regional banks, so I took a contract role there, which ended up being for 2 years. Last year, they made me permanent with a VP role. It was a different environment than working for an IT company, and I found the environment quite boring. I sometimes had run-ins with other colleagues because they used a self-entitled "but I am a VP, so you need to respect me more" mindset. But shit, look around everyone is a VP of something. But it was good because it helped me set some clearer direction, and I got 2 years of extra $$$ breathing space. I was happy to walk away from that, aged 43, and now I considered myself retired. A couple of years later, another ex-colleague rings me up and I take on a 100-day consulting contract for an Indian telecommunication company. Well, that was super interesting because, as a very transparent consultant, they didn't like my recommendations on what they needed to do to get their multiple projects back on schedule, budget and specification. Too much internal politics for them to decide who to fire. I spent about 60 of those days working on site and the last 40 days at home doing about 2 hours per day. That was my last career-related job, so October 2014 was my last day of work. I haven't worked since. Yay!

What did I invest in?

OK, the main investment timeline is something like the following: And unlike someone who has just been to the horse races or casino, I will tell you the shit ones too. It's amazing how we only hear about the wins – human ego again? or maybe they just can't see it.

In my first job at 18, someone sold me on investing in something I don't recall. I think it was designed to set me up for a pension. I stopped adding to it when I left NZ.

In my 20s, I mainly had bank fixed-term deposits. Didn't know any better.

At 31, I bought some mutual funds. I only held them for a few years then sold them but made about 5%. I wonder what they would be worth today?

At 32, I bought some stocks behind the big tech hype. Yes, I got burnt in the dot.com bubble and sold out. It kept me away from the stock market for many years and kept me focused on property. Shame I didn't learn about compounding and dollar cost averaging back then!

At 32 onwards, property focused: I bought my first property in Australia (sold for profit) and then probably every 2 years after that some more property: some land in NZ (sold for profit), then a property in Spain (sold for loss) and then property in NZ (sold for loss) and then in Bali (sold for profit) and then in NZ (sold for loss) and then in Singapore (sold for profit) and then in Bali (sold for loss) and NZ (sold for profit) and then in Singapore (sold for loss) and then in Singapore (sold for profit) and then some land in Australia (sold for loss). I still hold some property in NZ and Thailand.

At 49, I invested back into the stock markets and, to date, doing well.

Overall, I gained from the property investments but learnt some valuable lessons:

- Only sell property when you have to (a divorce meant I had to force sell some property = ouch).
- Don't buy property on the back of emotion (the thought of having a property in Spain and Bali was way cooler than the reality).
- A couple of those losses weren't net losses, as rental income gained over the years offset the loss in the property sale.
- Don't buy in an area where you will get shit tenants (a NZ experience referenced earlier).
- Never sell property? If I still had those properties, I am pretty sure my net worth (and my passive income) would be higher than today (although it is hard to tell exactly because I sold some property to buy another property or I took some property capital and invested into the stock markets).

I am pleased I have been investing since my early 30s, but I wish I could've started in my early 20s – **Shit no one taught me.**

I am pleased I never went super high risk on a single investment – it meant I could keep moving forward.

I don't bother with the hindsight "if only game." oh, I should've bought Bitcoin at $1. The only hindsight I regret is that I didn't understand the power of making my money work for me. If I knew about compounding returns and the power of patience I think the road would have been smoother. The simplest thing I would've changed was to have started investing in some index ETFs and just dollar cost averaged every quarter (and also build up a long-term property portfolio), but when I started, it wasn't easy to just buy an ETF online. It's certainly easier these days, and if I had kids, that's what I would be doing for their birthdays.

My current portfolio:

Mine is a little more complex than most, but that is primarily because I don't really have a natural base currency. If for example, I lived in New Zealand and planned to live in New Zealand for the rest of my life, and given the NZD is traditionally a relatively stable currency, then I would likely make the NZD my base currency. I live in Thailand, and the Thai Baht isn't super strong at times, so I don't invest within Thailand. Over the years I have earnt Stirling and Hong Kong Dollars and predominantly Singapore Dollars.

But essentially, it's roughly something like:

Cash (mostly earning low interest = passive income in NZD).

Property (capital gains growth and rental passive income in NZD)

Stocks/ETFs (growth and passive income from dividends). My ETFs (typically index-tracking ETFs) make up about 40% of this portfolio, and I will slowly increase this to >50% over the next few years).

Of my Stock/ETFS, it is roughly

65% USD based

10% Euro based

23% AUD based.

2% SGD based

< 1% speculation (I don't need to risk any more than this)

I don't have cash flow issues due to the passive income, so I don't have to panic sell in events like Covid.

Above works for me as it does give me currency diversification in case any one of the above really shits itself and/or one of the above goes through the roof. And when I travel, I can decide which one to spend.

I'm not sure how typical a portfolio like the above is for someone my age, but I am comfortable that it is balanced enough and will slowly de-risk it as I get older - although I think it will likely de-risk itself as I expect my dividends will continue to grow simply due to the length of time I will be holding them – each year my passive income grows. In summary;

- I have emergency cash.
- I have nothing big to buy over the next 5 years'ish
- My passive income easily exceeds my cost of living.
- My passive income grows more than inflation.
- My growth (although not always in a straight line) is good growth.
- I don't high risk/high reward >1% of my portfolio.
- I am balanced/I am diversified.
- I have financial breathing space.
- I have Financial Freedom.

CLOSING REMARKS.

My approach to Financial Freedom has never been a super high-risk scheme. I basically worked hard and then added smart and saved my money (managed my expenses) and then invested along the way (but starting really in my 30s) and retired at 43 (officially'ish). But most important, I had a plan – a very boring Excel spreadsheet, but that helped to keep me focused. Matching that up with some cool hobbies and Financial Freedom works very well for me.

I hope you have enjoyed my journey and that my recommendations, experience, and anecdotes help you along your Financial Freedom journey. It's very rewarding and FUN. Super good luck!!

And hopefully, in a few years from now, people all over the world will be yelling from the rooftops.

"FINANCIAL FREEDOM – SHIT SOMEONE TAUGHT US FINALLY!!!!"

And........

May the force of compounding be with you!

WHAT NEXT?

For you: Create your forever Financial Freedom road map, make your money work for you, and address those uncomfortable decisions!

For me: I quite enjoyed writing this book (finally). Financial Freedom is a topic I am probably most passionate about and most frustrated with the education system over. As I type, this book is still in rough draft, so I now have to navigate how to get it reviewed, edited, cover designed, published, marketed...so that's good as I will learn some new things. (If you are reading this book, then yes, I worked it out). If the book takes off, then that's great. If not, I now have something I can hand to people I meet (instead of my not-so-great elevator pitch). If the opportunity does arise, then I would be happy to do presentations and maybe workshops on this (maybe I will even get offered a TED TALK - come on, Ted, you know you want me!). But the ideal perfect outcome is this goes super viral, and schools wake up and start building this into their curriculum. And parents also wake up and learn this stuff and then start teaching it to their kids. It would be interesting to find out if global economies collapse because consumerism would shrink if everyone adopted my tight arse behaviour. Many corporations would need to rethink their product BRAND pitch. Would the world be a better place if everyone found their Financial Freedom focus? I play this scenario outcome through when cycling sometimes – my conclusion is we end up with a more balanced society and less taxes (Government spending on the elderly reduces as they are financially free/less social welfare payment/less diabetes/less lung cancer, etc.). Netflix, please sign me up for the sci-fi version of this!

I do have a couple of other book topics I would like to have a crack at, so this book hopefully becomes a good catalyst for that as it's a good way to keep the brain active in retirement: and Cool Brain can remain Cool and not hit me with Dementia.

If you want to reach out to me, then you can email me at waynesweet07@gmail.com.

I am happy to help where possible and would be interested in hearing about your own journey experiences. (Remember to reach out in a constructive way).

If you want to help me, then **please do a book review on Amazon,** as apparently, that's the main algorithm driver for which books are rated/promoted.

ACKNOWLEDGEMENTS.

No single person stands out – just many different people along the way who I have taken (or not taken) advice and guidance from. Many events have probably impacted me without knowing how they may have influenced my decision processes. We can't pinpoint why each decision is made in life and why we turn out the way we do (nurture versus nature). I thank my older brother for mentoring me on how to steal milk bottle money and I thank Mum for wanting to smack me around for buying a bottle of fizzy drink.

So, in essence, there is a little bit of thanks to everyone – and thanks to my school teachers - sorry I was such a shit listener!!

Big thanks to Dave, Eedy, Jen, Alastair, OB, Sue, Tom and Luca for the honest review feedback – much appreciated.

Special thanks to Eeeeedy for being a cool, patient, and fun partner! Your journey is super inspiring!

Finally, my idiot brain said I had to thank it and also said I have to stop calling it 'idiot,' so out of respect, I would like to say thank you, Cool Brain!!

Thanks, everyone, for being SUPER AWESOME

APPENDIX STUFF.

Index – No need for that.

Glossary – No need for that (E=MC2: Some Einstein thingy).

Book Dedication – No need for that.

Other books by Wayne Sweet = Zero.

OK, I wasn't going to list out the 39 guiding principles because I thought that would mean you would cheat and just skim-read for the 'secret Sweetie science' to Financial Freedom. But given there is no 'secret Sweetie science', there isn't really anything to cheat on, and I am trying to get over my trust issues. Hopefully, having them listed here will make a good quick 'YEP, I remember that' reference.

1. Don't use the word RXXX. It means nothing.
2. Financial Freedom means different things to different people - what does it mean for you?
3. Happiness versus Contentment.
4. Create a personal Financial Freedom plan and maintain it FOREVER!
5. Make decisions based on numbers – NOT EMOTION.
6. Professional Financial Advisers ALWAYS(?) have a product to sell.
7. Get RXXX quick =s SCAM!
8. It's not a sprint – it's a marathon!
9. Time goes quicker than you may realise. Patience is key.
10. Greed is a killer.
11. Kiss Your EGO Goodbye!
12. Consumerism: Needs vs Wants – It's all just STUFF!
13. Smart versus Patience versus Luck.

14. Higher risk profile when younger – lower risk profile when older.
15. Understand Return on Investment (ROI).
16. Understand the power of compounding returns.
17. Understand the power of 2nd, 3rd, 4th, 5th+ + income streams.
18. Take advantage of investment tax benefits.
19. Assume no Government pension when you retire:
20. Understand Good Debt versus Bad Debt!
21. Is a University degree good debt or bad debt??
22. Career Choice: Chase your passion or chase the money ladder.
23. Will your career be relevant (in demand) in 5, 10, 15, or 20 years?
24. Invest in things you understand and are interested in.
25. Balance your portfolio.
26. Read lots, but not everything you read is gospel.
27. Talk 'investing' with others: It doesn't have to be Taboo!!
28. Be a saver - not a spender.
29. Don't be too much of a Tight Arse.
30. Never loan money to friends/family WITHOUT a loan agreement with penalties.
31. Have a Will and understand your inheritance tax.
32. Insurances – cover yourself.
33. Is having children good for your Financial Freedom plan?
34. Plan as a couple.
35. Stay away from negative people!
36. Don't play the victim.
37. Self-motivation is key.
38. Don't limit goals to just financial goals.
39. It's your turn to add some guiding principles.

WOOOOHOOOOOO

The very cool shit completed its journey and achieved Financial Freedom...

Well done! Congratulations!

I am very proud of you!!

I hope no one is offended by my use of shit - it just seemed like a fun way to connect "shit no one teaches us" with something fun (in a serious book). If my Leonardo AI image is a bit puke for you, then just re-imagine it as a scoop of chocolate ice cream achieving its Financial Freedom = problem solved!!

The mechanics of writing this book:

Below is an email I sent to my good friend Dave in Singapore, who has been a massive help with the book as my original introductions were a bit crap, and he has been great to sound-board ideas off. This email was about deciding which 'shit' to have on the cover and at the end.

Hey Dave

What about this shit? I will soften up the edges on the white background, blending with the jpeg.

But I think it shows a young, optimistic shit looking forward to learning about financial freedom, and the hat makes it seem a little more human/relevant?

The second shit will be right at the end of the book. In this email, they are right next to each other, and they clearly look like different shits...

I will try and make the second shit look more like the first shit if I can work out how to do that in Leonardo ai. and it could do with losing some weight; otherwise, the readers might think part of achieving financial freedom is to turn into a big shit.

And I might remove the $$ $$ as that's not my style... if I can't remove the $$, then I probably make a joke about how the shits gone bling on us and now thinks it's a gangsta shit...

makes sense

Cheers, Wayne (sorry for talking so much shit!)

(Needless to say, based on the above 'big shit' picture, I couldn't work out Leonard AI too well, but also, I kinda got attached to the 'big shit' image that AI created – and he's not really a gangsta shit!!)

OK, the book mechanics was pretty simple – eventually. Once I was committed to making this project happen, I made sure that every day after lunch, I would contribute to the book. Sometimes it would be 1 hour, and sometimes it would be up to 4 hours. No strict number of hours per day process. Because it's based on my actual journey/knowledge, I spent virtually no time doing research, and I think that made the book writing experience more enjoyable. I watched quite a few YouTube videos on how to self-publish, and that has been very useful and important in giving me the confidence that I can get this book self-published. The original introduction I wrote was quite crap, but that's because I wrote the introduction and then the book content but never went back to re-write the introduction, so that was a good lesson learnt. If you think this final one is crap, well, you should've seen the first one.

I got positive, constructive comments from some friendly reviewers, which helped me shuffle some things around, but I also received positive affirmation to get this book out there.

My ROI = I will have spent USD220 on the 3rd party editing and book formatting. I probably need to sell 220 books for a positive ROI. If you are on Amazon and after 2 years see that this book hasn't sold very well, then I got a bad ROI from it (although not everything can be measured that way as I have gained a lot of satisfaction and knowledge out of this project).

They say to write a book, you need to be in a good physical space. Well, my space is lying back on my couch with my feet up and the laptop on my lap, and I look out over my balcony. Pretty chilled!

THE END!

Printed in Great Britain
by Amazon